Let's Keep in Touch

Follow Us   Online

Visit US at   https://www.facebook.com/Effortlessmath

www.EffortlessMath.com   https://goo.gl/2B6qWW

Online Math Lessons

It's easy! Here's how it works.

1- Request a FREE introductory session.
2- Meet a Math tutor online.
3- Start Learning Math in Minutes.

Send Email to: info@EffortlessMath.com

www.EffortlessMath.com

... So Much More Online!

- FREE Math lessons

- More Math learning books!

- Online Math Tutors

Looking for an Online Math Tutor?

Need a PDF format of this book?

Send Email to: info@EffortlessMath.com

ACCUPLACER Math
in
7 Days

Step–By–Step Guide to Preparing for the ACCUPLACER Math Test Quickly

By

Reza Nazari & Ava Ross

Copyright © 2018

Reza Nazari & Ava Ross

All rights reserved. No part of this publication may be reproduced, stored in a retrieval system, or transmitted in any form or by any means, electronic, mechanical, photocopying, recording, scanning, or otherwise, except as permitted under Section 107 or 108 of the 1976 United States Copyright Ac, without permission of the author.

All inquiries should be addressed to:

info@effortlessMath.com

www.EffortlessMath.com

ISBN-13: 978-1720431039

ISBN-10: 1720431035

Published by: Effortless Math Education

www.EffortlessMath.com

Description

The goal of this book is simple. It will help you incorporate the best method and the right strategies to prepare for the ACCUPLACER Math FAST and EFFECTIVELY.

ACCUPLACER Math in 7 Days is full of specific and detailed material that will be key to succeeding on the ACCUPLACER Math. It's filled with the critical math concepts a student will need in order to pass the test. Math concepts in this book break down the topics, so the material can be quickly grasped. Examples are worked step–by–step, so you learn exactly what to do.

ACCUPLACER Math in 7 Days helps you to focus on all Math topics that you will need to pass the ACCUPLACER Math test. You only need to spend about 3 – 4 hours daily in your 7–day period in order to pass the test. This book with 2 complete ACCUPLACER tests is all you will ever need to fully prepare for the ACCUPLACER Math.

This workbook includes practice test questions. It contains easy–to–read essential summaries that highlight the key areas of the ACCUPLACER Math test. Effortless Math test study guide reviews the most important components of the ACCUPLACER Math test. Anyone planning to take the ACCUPLACER Math test should take advantage of the review material and practice test questions contained in this study guide.

Whether you are intimidated by math, or even if you were the first to raise your hand in the Math classes, this book can help you accelerate the learning process and put you on the right track.

Inside the pages of this workbook, students can learn basic math operations in a structured manner with a complete study program to help them understand essential math skills. It also has many exciting features, including:

- Dynamic design and easy–to–follow activities
- A fun, interactive and concrete learning process
- Targeted, skill–building practices
- Math topics are grouped by category, so you can focus on the topics you struggle on

- All solutions for the exercises are included, so you will always find the answers
- 2 Complete ACCUPLACER Math Practice Tests that reflect the format and question types on ACCUPLACER

ACCUPLACER Math in 7 Days is a breakthrough in Math learning — offering a winning formula and the most powerful methods for learning basic Math topics confidently. Each section offers step–by–step instruction and helpful hints, with a few topics being tackled each day. Two complete REAL ACCUPLACER Math tests are provided at the back of the book to refine your Math skills.

Effortlessly and confidently follow the step–by–step instructions in this book to prepare for the ACCUPLACER Math in a short period of time.

ACCUPLACER Math in 7 Days **is the only book you'll ever need to master Basic Math topics!** It can be used as a self–study course – you do not need to work with a Math tutor. (It can also be used with a Math tutor).

You'll be surprised how fast you master the Math topics covering on ACCUPLACER Math Test.

Ideal for self–study as well as for classroom usage.

About the Author

Reza Nazari is the author of more than 100 Math learning books including:
– **Math and Critical Thinking Challenges:** For the Middle and High School Student
– **GRE Math in 30 Days.**
– **ASVAB Math Workbook 2018 – 2019**
– **Effortless Math Education Workbooks**
– and many more Mathematics books ...

Reza is also an experienced Math instructor and a test–prep expert who has been tutoring students since 2008. Reza is the founder of Effortless Math Education, a tutoring company that has helped many students raise their standardized test scores—and attend the colleges of their dreams. Reza provides an individualized custom learning plan and the personalized attention that makes a difference in how students view math.

To ask questions about Math, you can contact Reza via email at:
reza@EffortlessMath.com

Find Reza's professional profile at:
goo.gl/zoC9rJ

Contents

Day 1: Fundamentals and Building Blocks 11

- Simplifying Fractions 12
- Adding and Subtracting Fractions 13
- Multiplying and Dividing Fractions 14
- Adding Mixed Numbers 15
- Subtract Mixed Numbers 16
- Multiplying Mixed Numbers 17
- Dividing Mixed Numbers 18
- Comparing Decimals 19
- Rounding Decimals 20
- Adding and Subtracting Decimals 21
- Multiplying and Dividing Decimals 22
- Converting Between Fractions, Decimals and Mixed Numbers 23
- Factoring Numbers 24
- Greatest Common Factor 25
- Least Common Multiple 26
- Adding and Subtracting Integers 27
- Multiplying and Dividing Integers 28
- Answers of Worksheets – Day 1 29

Day 2: Proportions and Variables 35

- Ordering Integers and Numbers 36
- Arrange, Order, and Comparing Integers 37
- Order of Operations 38
- Mixed Integer Computations 39
- Integers and Absolute Value 40
- Writing Ratios 41
- Simplifying Ratios 42
- Create a Proportion 43
- Similar Figures 44
- Simple Interest 45
- Ratio and Rates Word Problems 46

- Percentage Calculations..47
- Converting Between Percent, Fractions, and Decimals...............................48
- Percent Problems..49
- Markup, Discount, and Tax 50
- Expressions and Variables..51
- Simplifying Variable Expressions...52
- Simplifying Polynomial Expressions..53
- Translate Phrases into an Algebraic Statement 54
- Answers of Worksheets – Day 3..55

Day 3: Equations and Inequalities..60
- The Distributive Property...61
- Evaluating One Variable...62
- Evaluating Two Variables...63
- Combining like Terms...64
- One–Step Equations..65
- Two–Step Equations..66
- Multi–Step Equations..67
- Graphing Single–Variable Inequalities..68
- One–Step Inequalities...69
- Two–Step Inequalities...70
- Multi–Step Inequalities...71
- Finding Slope...72
- Graphing Lines Using Slope–Intercept Form..73
- Graphing Lines Using Standard Form...74
- Writing Linear Equations..75
- Graphing Linear Inequalities..76
- Finding Midpoint...77
- Finding Distance of Two Points...78
- Answers of Worksheets – Day 4..79

Day 4: Monomials and Polynomials...86
- Classifying Polynomials..87
- Writing Polynomials in Standard Form...88

Simplifying Polynomials 89

Adding and Subtracting Polynomials 90

Multiplying Monomials 91

Multiplying and Dividing Monomials 92

Multiplying a Polynomial and a Monomial 93

Multiplying Binomials 94

Factoring Trinomials 95

Operations with Polynomials 96

Solve a Quadratic Equation 97

Is (x, y) a solution to the system of equations? 98

Solving Systems of Equations 99

Answers of Worksheets – Day 5 100

Day 5: Exponents, Roots and Statistics 104

Multiplication Property of Exponents 105

Division Property of Exponents 106

Powers of Products and Quotients 107

Zero and Negative Exponents 108

Negative Exponents and Negative Bases 109

Writing Scientific Notation 110

Square Roots 111

Mean, Median, Mode, and Range of the Given Data 112

Box and Whisker Plots 113

Bar Graph 114

Stem–And–Leaf Plot 115

The Pie Graph or Circle Graph 116

Scatter Plots 117

Probability Problems 118

Answers of Worksheets – Day 6 119

Day 6: Geometry 124

The Pythagorean Theorem 125

Area of Triangles 126

Perimeter of Polygons 127

Area and Circumference of Circles...128

Area of Squares, Rectangles, and Parallelograms..129

Area of Trapezoids 130

Volume of Cubes 131

Volume of Rectangle Prisms 132

Surface Area of Cubes 133

Surface Area of a Rectangle Prism 134

Volume of a Cylinder 135

Surface Area of a Cylinder 136

Answers of Worksheets – Day 7 137

Day 7: Geometry and Conic Sections 139

Sketch Each Angle in Standard Position...140

Finding Co–Terminal Angles and Reference Angles..141

Writing Each Measure in Radians 142

Writing Each Measure in Degrees..143

Evaluating Each Trigonometric 144

Missing Sides and Angles of a Right Triangle 145

Arc Length and Sector Area 146

Trig Ratios of General Angles..147

Finding the Focus, Vertex, and Directrix of a Parabola...148

Writing the Standard Form of a Circle 149

Finding the Center and the Radius of Circles 150

Arithmetic Sequences 151

Geometric Sequences 152

Answers of Worksheets – Day 7 153

ACCUPLACER Mathematics Practice Tests...159

Time to Test 160

ACCUPLACER Mathematics Practice Test 1 161

ACCUPLACER Mathematics Practice Test 2 176

ACCUPLACER Math Practice Test 1 Answer Key 191

ACCUPLACER Math Practice Test 2 Answer Key 192

ACCUPLACER Mathematics Practice Test 1 Answers and Explanations 194

ACCUPLACER Mathematics Practice Test 2 Answers and Explanations 202

Day 1: Fundamentals and Building Blocks

Math Topics that you'll learn today:

- ~~Simplifying Fractions~~
- Adding and Subtracting Fractions
- Multiplying and Dividing Fractions
- Adding Mixed Numbers
- Subtracting Mixed Numbers
- Multiplying Mixed Numbers
- Dividing Mixed Numbers
- Comparing Decimals
- Rounding Decimals
- Adding and Subtracting Decimals
- Multiplying and Dividing Decimals
- Converting Between Fractions, Decimals and Mixed Numbers
- Divisibility Rules
- Factoring Numbers
- Greatest Common Factor
- Least Common Multiple
- Adding and Subtracting Integers
- Multiplying and Dividing Integers

"If people do not believe that mathematics is simple, it is only because they do not realize how complicated life is." — John von Neumann

Simplifying Fractions

Helpful Hints
- Evenly divide both the top and bottom of the fraction by 2, 3, 5, 7, ... etc.
- Continue until you can't go any further.

Example:
$$\frac{4}{12} = \frac{2}{6} = \frac{1}{3}$$

*go over prime #'s

✍ Simplify the fractions.

1) $\frac{22}{36} = \frac{11}{18}$

2) $\frac{8}{10} = \frac{4}{5}$

3) $\frac{12}{18} = \frac{6}{9} = \frac{2}{3}$

4) $\frac{6}{8} = \frac{3}{4}$

5) $\frac{13}{39}$

6) $\frac{5}{20} = \frac{1}{4}$

7) $\frac{16}{36} = \frac{4}{9}$

8) $\frac{18}{36} = \frac{9}{18} = \frac{1}{2}$

9) $\frac{20}{50} = \frac{4}{10} = \frac{2}{5}$

10) $\frac{6}{54} = \frac{1}{9}$

11) $\frac{45}{81} = \frac{5}{9}$

12) $\frac{21}{28} = \frac{3}{4}$

13) $\frac{35}{56} = \frac{5}{8}$

14) $\frac{52}{64} = \frac{26}{32} = \frac{13}{16}$

15) $\frac{13}{65}$

16) $\frac{44}{77} = \frac{4}{7}$

17) $\frac{21}{42} = \frac{3}{6} = \frac{1}{2}$

18) $\frac{15}{36}$

19) $\frac{9}{24} = \frac{3}{8}$

20) $\frac{20}{80} = \frac{2}{8} = \frac{1}{4}$

21) $\frac{25}{45} = \frac{5}{9}$

ACCUPLACER Math in 7 Days

Adding and Subtracting Fractions

WATCH YOUTUBE OVER

Helpful Hints

— For "like" fractions (fractions with the same denominator), add or subtract the numerators and write the answer over the common denominator.
— Find equivalent fractions with the same denominator before you can add or subtract fractions with different denominators.
— Adding and Subtracting with the same denominator:

$$\frac{a}{b} + \frac{c}{b} = \frac{a+c}{b}$$
$$\frac{a}{b} - \frac{c}{b} = \frac{a-c}{b}$$

— Adding and Subtracting fractions with different denominators:

$$\frac{a}{b} + \frac{c}{d} = \frac{ad+cb}{bd}$$
$$\frac{a}{b} - \frac{c}{d} = \frac{ad-cb}{bd}$$

Add fractions.

1) $\frac{2}{3} + \frac{1}{2} = \frac{4+3}{6} = \frac{7}{6}$?

2) $\frac{3}{5} + \frac{1}{3} = \frac{9+5}{8} = \frac{14}{8}$

3) $\frac{5}{6} + \frac{1}{2} = \frac{10+6}{12} = \frac{10}{12}$

4) $\frac{7}{4} + \frac{5}{9}$

5) $\frac{2}{5} + \frac{1}{5}$

6) $\frac{3}{7} + \frac{1}{2}$

7) $\frac{3}{4} + \frac{2}{5}$

8) $\frac{2}{3} + \frac{1}{5}$

9) $\frac{16}{25} + \frac{3}{5}$

Subtract fractions.

10) $\frac{4}{5} - \frac{2}{5}$

11) $\frac{3}{5} - \frac{2}{7}$

12) $\frac{1}{2} - \frac{1}{3}$

13) $\frac{8}{9} - \frac{3}{5}$

14) $\frac{3}{7} - \frac{3}{14}$

15) $\frac{4}{15} - \frac{1}{10}$

16) $\frac{3}{4} - \frac{13}{18}$

17) $\frac{5}{8} - \frac{2}{5}$

18) $\frac{1}{2} - \frac{1}{9}$

www.EffortlessMath.com

Multiplying and Dividing Fractions

Helpful Hints

— **Multiplying fractions:** multiply the top numbers and multiply the bottom numbers.
— **Dividing fractions:** Keep, Change, Flip
Keep first fraction, change division sign to multiplication, and flip the numerator and denominator of the second fraction. Then, solve!

Example:
$$\frac{a}{b} \times \frac{c}{d} = \frac{a \times c}{b \times d}$$

$$\frac{a}{b} \div \frac{c}{d} = \frac{a}{b} \times \frac{d}{c} = \frac{ad}{bc}$$

✎ *Multiplying fractions. Then simplify.*

1) $\frac{1}{5} \times \frac{2}{3}$

2) $\frac{3}{4} \times \frac{2}{3}$

3) $\frac{2}{5} \times \frac{3}{7}$

4) $\frac{3}{8} \times \frac{1}{3}$

5) $\frac{3}{5} \times \frac{2}{5}$

6) $\frac{7}{9} \times \frac{1}{3}$

7) $\frac{2}{3} \times \frac{3}{8}$

8) $\frac{1}{4} \times \frac{1}{3}$

9) $\frac{5}{7} \times \frac{7}{12}$

✎ *Dividing fractions.*

10) $\frac{2}{9} \div \frac{1}{4}$

11) $\frac{1}{2} \div \frac{1}{3}$

12) $\frac{6}{11} \div \frac{3}{4}$

13) $\frac{11}{14} \div \frac{1}{10}$

14) $\frac{3}{5} \div \frac{5}{9}$

15) $\frac{1}{2} \div \frac{1}{2}$

16) $\frac{3}{5} \div \frac{1}{5}$

17) $\frac{12}{21} \div \frac{3}{7}$

18) $\frac{5}{14} \div \frac{9}{10}$

Adding Mixed Numbers

Helpful Hints

Use the following steps for both adding and subtracting mixed numbers.

– Find the Least Common Denominator (LCD)
– Find the equivalent fractions for each mixed number.
– Add fractions after finding common denominator.
– Write your answer in lowest terms.

Example:

$1\frac{3}{4} + 2\frac{3}{8} = 4\frac{1}{8}$

✎ Add.

1) $4\frac{1}{2} + 5\frac{1}{2}$

2) $2\frac{3}{8} + 3\frac{1}{8}$

3) $6\frac{1}{5} + 3\frac{2}{5}$

4) $1\frac{1}{3} + 2\frac{2}{3}$

5) $5\frac{1}{6} + 5\frac{1}{2}$

6) $3\frac{1}{3} + 1\frac{1}{3}$

7) $1\frac{10}{11} + 1\frac{1}{3}$

8) $2\frac{3}{6} + 1\frac{1}{2}$

9) $5\frac{3}{5} + 5\frac{1}{5}$

10) $7 + \frac{1}{5}$

11) $1\frac{5}{7} + \frac{1}{3}$

12) $2\frac{1}{4} + 1\frac{1}{2}$

Subtract Mixed Numbers

Helpful Hints

Use the following steps for both adding and subtracting mixed numbers.

Find the Least Common Denominator (LCD)
— Find the equivalent fractions for each mixed number.
— Add or subtract fractions after finding common denominator.
— Write your answer in lowest terms.

Example:

$5\frac{2}{3} - 3\frac{2}{7} = 2\frac{8}{21}$

✏️ Subtract.

1) $4\frac{1}{2} - 3\frac{1}{2}$

2) $3\frac{3}{8} - 3\frac{1}{8}$

3) $6\frac{3}{5} - 5\frac{1}{5}$

4) $2\frac{1}{3} - 1\frac{2}{3}$

5) $6\frac{1}{6} - 5\frac{1}{2}$

6) $3\frac{1}{3} - 1\frac{1}{3}$

7) $2\frac{10}{11} - 1\frac{1}{3}$

8) $2\frac{1}{2} - 1\frac{1}{2}$

9) $6\frac{3}{5} - 2\frac{1}{5}$

10) $7\frac{2}{5} - 1\frac{1}{5}$

11) $2\frac{5}{7} - 1\frac{1}{3}$

12) $2\frac{1}{4} - 1\frac{1}{2}$

Multiplying Mixed Numbers

Helpful Hints

1- Convert the mixed numbers to improper fractions.
2- Multiply fractions and simplify if necessary.

$$a\frac{c}{b} = a + \frac{c}{b} = \frac{ab\ c}{b}$$

Example:

$$2\frac{1}{3} \times 5\frac{3}{7} =$$

$$\frac{7}{3} \times \frac{38}{7} = \frac{38}{3} = 12\frac{2}{3}$$

✎ Find each product.

1) $1\frac{2}{3} \times 1\frac{1}{4}$

2) $1\frac{3}{5} \times 1\frac{2}{3}$

3) $1\frac{2}{3} \times 3\frac{2}{7}$

4) $4\frac{1}{8} \times 1\frac{2}{5}$

5) $2\frac{2}{5} \times 3\frac{1}{5}$

6) $1\frac{1}{3} \times 1\frac{2}{3}$

7) $1\frac{5}{8} \times 2\frac{1}{2}$

8) $3\frac{2}{5} \times 2\frac{1}{5}$

9) $2\frac{2}{3} \times 4\frac{1}{4}$

10) $2\frac{3}{5} \times 1\frac{2}{4}$

11) $1\frac{1}{3} \times 1\frac{1}{4}$

12) $3\frac{2}{5} \times 1\frac{1}{5}$

Dividing Mixed Numbers

Helpful Hints

1- Convert the mixed numbers to improper fractions.
2- Divide fractions and simplify if necessary.

$$a\frac{c}{b} = a + \frac{c}{b} = \frac{ab+c}{b}$$

Example:

$$2\frac{1}{3} \times 5\frac{3}{7} =$$

$$\frac{7}{3} \times \frac{38}{7} = \frac{38}{3} = 12\frac{2}{3}$$

✎ Find each quotient.

1) $2\frac{1}{5} \div 2\frac{1}{2}$

2) $2\frac{3}{5} \div 1\frac{1}{3}$

3) $3\frac{1}{6} \div 4\frac{2}{3}$

4) $1\frac{2}{3} \div 3\frac{1}{3}$

5) $4\frac{1}{8} \div 2\frac{2}{4}$

6) $3\frac{1}{2} \div 2\frac{3}{5}$

7) $3\frac{5}{9} \div 1\frac{2}{5}$

8) $2\frac{2}{7} \div 1\frac{1}{2}$

9) $3\frac{1}{5} \div 1\frac{1}{2}$

10) $4\frac{3}{5} \div 2\frac{1}{3}$

11) $6\frac{1}{6} \div 1\frac{2}{3}$

12) $2\frac{2}{3} \div 1\frac{1}{3}$

Comparing Decimals

Helpful Hints

- **Decimals:** is a fraction written in a special form. For example, instead of writing $\frac{1}{2}$ you can write 0.5.
- **For comparing:**
  Equal to =
  Less than <
  Greater than >
  Greater than or equal ≥
  Less than or equal ≤

Example:

2.67 > 0.267

✎ Write the correct comparison symbol (>, < or =).

1) 1.25 < 2.3

2) 0.5 > 0.23

3) 3.2 = 3.2

4) 4.58 < 45.8

5) 2.75 > 0.275

6) 5.2 > 5

7) 3.1 > 0.31

8) 6.33 > 0.733

9) 8 > 0.8

10) 4.56 > 0.456

11) 1.12 < 1.14

12) 2.77 < 2.78

13) 6.08 < 6.11

14) 1.11 > 0.211

15) 2.6 > 2.55

16) 1.24 < 1.25

17) 5.52 > 0.552

18) 0.33 > 0.033

19) 14.4 = 14.4

20) 0.05 < 0.50

21) 0.59 < 0.7

22) 0.5 > 0.05

23) 0.90 = 0.90

24) 0.2 < 0.4

ACCUPLACER Math in 7 Days

Rounding Decimals   DOUBLE CHECK

Helpful Hints

We can round decimals to a certain accuracy or number of decimal places. This is used to make calculation easier to do and results easier to understand, when exact values are not too important.

First, you'll need to remember your place values:

Example:

6.37 = 6

12.4567

1: tens 2: ones 4: tenths

5: hundredths 6: thousandths 7: tens thousandths

✎ **Round each decimal number to the nearest place indicated.**

1) 0.23 = 0.2

2) 4.04 = 4

3) 5.623 = 6

4) 0.266 = 0

5) 6.37 = 6

6) 0.88 = 1

7) 8.24 = 8

8) 7.0760 = 7

9) 1.629 = 1.60

10) 6.3959 = 6

11) 1.9 = 2

12) 5.2167 = 5

13) 5.863 = 6

14) 8.54 = 8.50

15) 80.69 = 81

16) 65.85 = 66

17) 70.78 = 71

18) 615.755 = 616

19) 16.4 = 16

20) 95.81 = 96

21) 2.408 = 2

22) 76.3 = 76

23) 116.514 = 116

24) 8.06 = 8

20 www.EffortlessMath.com

ACCUPLACER Math in 7 Days YOUTUBE

Adding and Subtracting Decimals

Helpful Hints

1– Line up the numbers.

2– Add zeros to have same number of digits for both numbers.

3– Add or Subtract using column addition or subtraction.

Example:

```
   16.18
 − 13.45
   2.73
```

✎ Add and subtract decimals.

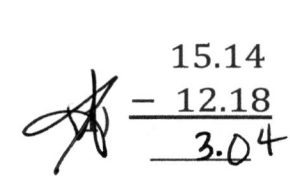

1) 15.14
   − 12.18
   ──────
     3.04

3) 82.56
   + 12.28
   ──────

5) 90.37
   + 56.97
   ──────

2) 65.72
   + 43.67
   ──────

4) 34.18
   − 23.45
   ──────

6) 45.78
   − 23.39
   ──────

✎ Solve.

7) ____ + 1.3 = 4.8

8) 4.2 + ____ = 11.6

9) 9.9 + ____ = 16

10) 6.9 + ____ = 16.4

11) ____ + 5.1 = 8.6

12) ____ + 7.9 = 15.2

Multiplying and Dividing Decimals

Helpful Hints

For Multiplication:

− Set up and multiply the numbers as you do with whole numbers.

− Count the total number of decimal places in both of the factors.

− Place the decimal point in the product.

For Division:

− If the divisor is not a whole number, move decimal point to right to make it a whole number. Do the same for dividend.

− Divide similar to whole numbers.

✍ **Find each product.**

1) 4.5 × 1.6

2) 7.7 × 9.9

3) 2.6 × 1.5

4) 8.9 × 9.7

5) 15.1 × 12.6

6) 6.9 × 3.3

7) 5.7 × 7.8

8) 98.20 × 100

9) 23.99 × 1000

✍ **Find each quotient.**

10) 9.2 ÷ 3.6

11) 27.6 ÷ 3.8

12) 12.6 ÷ 4.7

13) 6.5 ÷ 8.1

14) 1.4 ÷ 10

15) 3.6 ÷ 100

16) 4.24 ÷ 10

17) 14.6 ÷ 100

18) 1.8 ÷ 1000

Converting Between Fractions, Decimals and Mixed Numbers

Helpful Hints

Fraction to Decimal:

− Divide the top number by the bottom number.

Decimal to Fraction:

− Write decimal over 1.

− Multiply both top and bottom by 10 for every digit on the right side of the decimal point.

− Simplify.

✎ Convert fractions to decimals.

1) $\dfrac{9}{10}$

2) $\dfrac{56}{100}$

3) $\dfrac{3}{4}$

4) $\dfrac{2}{5}$

5) $\dfrac{3}{9}$

6) $\dfrac{40}{50}$

7) $\dfrac{12}{10}$

8) $\dfrac{8}{5}$

9) $\dfrac{69}{10}$

✎ Convert decimal into fraction or mixed numbers.

10) 0.3

11) 4.5

12) 2.5

13) 2.3

14) 0.8

15) 0.25

16) 0.14

17) 0.2

18) 0.08

19) 0.45

20) 2.6

21) 5.2

ACCUPLACER Math in 7 Days

Factoring Numbers

Helpful Hints	- Factoring numbers means to break the numbers into their prime factors. - First few prime numbers: 2, 3, 5, 7, 11, 13, 17, 19	Example: $12 = 2 \times 2 \times 3$

✎ List all positive factors of each number.

1) 68

2) 56

3) 24 = 2, 4, 6, 8, 12,

4) 40 = 2, 4, 5, 8, 10, 20

5) 86

6) 78

7) 50 = 2, 5, 25, 10

8) 98

9) 45

10) 26

11) 54

12) 28

13) 55

14) 85

15) 48

✎ List the prime factorization for each number.

16) 50

17) 25

18) 69

19) 21

20) 45

21) 68

22) 26

23) 86

24) 93

24

www.EffortlessMath.com

Greatest Common Factor

Helpful Hints

- List the prime factors of each number.
- Multiply common prime factors.

Example:

$200 = 2 \times 2 \times 2 \times 5 \times 5$

$60 = 2 \times 2 \times 3 \times 5$

$GCF\ (200, 60) = 2 \times 2 \times 5 = 20$

✎ *Find the GCF for each number pair.*

1) 20, 30

2) 4, 14

3) 5, 45

4) 68, 12

5) 5, 12

6) 15, 27

7) 3, 24

8) 34, 6

9) 4, 10

10) 5, 3

11) 6, 16

12) 30, 3

13) 24, 28

14) 70, 10

15) 45, 8

16) 90, 35

17) 78, 34

18) 55, 75

19) 60, 72

20) 100, 78

21) 30, 40

Least Common Multiple

Helpful Hints
- Find the GCF for the two numbers.
- Divide that GCF into either number.
- Take that answer and multiply it by the other number.

Example:

LCM (200, 60):

GCF is 20

200 ÷ 20 = 10

10 × 60 = 600

✎ Find the LCM for each number pair.

1) 4, 14

2) 5, 15

3) 16, 10

4) 4, 34

5) 8, 3

6) 12, 24

7) 9, 18

8) 5, 6

9) 8, 19

10) 9, 21

11) 19, 29

12) 7, 6

13) 25, 6

14) 4, 8

15) 30, 10, 50

16) 18, 36, 27

17) 12, 8, 18

18) 8, 18, 4

19) 26, 20, 30

20) 10, 4, 24

21) 15, 30, 45

Adding and Subtracting Integers

Helpful Hints

- **Integers:** {... , −3, −2, −1, 0, 1, 2, 3, ...} Includes: zero, counting numbers, and the negative of the counting numbers.
- Add a positive integer by moving to the right on the number line.
- Add a negative integer by moving to the left on the number line.
- Subtract an integer by adding its opposite.

Example:

12 + 10 = 22

25 − 13 = 12

(−24) + 12 = −12

(−14) + (−12) = −26

14 − (−13) = 27

✎ Find the sum.

1) (− 12) + (− 4)

2) 5 + (− 24)

3) (− 14) + 23

4) (− 8) + (39)

5) 43 + (−12)

6) (− 23) + (− 4) + 3

7) 4 + (− 12) + (− 10) + (− 25)

8) 19 + (− 15) + 25 + 11

9) (− 9) + (− 12) + (32 − 14)

10) 4 + (− 30) + (45 − 34)

✎ Find the difference.

11) (− 14) − (− 9) − (18)

12) (− 9) − (− 25)

13) (− 12) − (8)

14) (28) − (− 4)

15) (34) − (2)

16) (55) − (− 5) + (− 4)

17) (9) − (2) − (− 5)

18) (2) − (4) − (− 15)

19) (23) − (4) − (− 34)

20) (− 45) − (− 87)

Multiplying and Dividing Integers

Helpful Hints

(negative) × (negative) = positive

(negative) ÷ (negative) = positive

(negative) × (positive) = negative

(negative) ÷ (positive) = negative

(positive) × (positive) = positive

Examples:

3 × 2 = 6

3 × − 3 = − 9

− 2 × − 2 = 4

10 ÷ 2 = 5

− 4 ÷ 2 = − 2

− 12 ÷ − 6 = 3

✎ **Find each product.**

1) (− 8) × (− 2)

2) 3 × 6

3) (− 4) × 5 × (− 6)

4) 2 × (− 6) × (− 6)

5) 11 × (− 12)

6) 10 × (− 5)

7) 8 × 8

8) (− 8) × (− 9)

9) 6 × (− 5) × 3

10) 6 × (− 1) × 2

✎ **Find each quotient.**

11) 18 ÷ 3

12) (− 24) ÷ 4

13) (− 63) ÷ (− 9)

14) 54 ÷ 9

15) 20 ÷ (− 2)

16) (− 66) ÷ (− 11)

17) 64 ÷ 8

18) (− 121) ÷ 11

19) 72 ÷ 9

20) 16 ÷ 4

Answers of Worksheets – Day 1

Simplifying Fractions

1) $\frac{11}{18}$
2) $\frac{4}{5}$
3) $\frac{2}{3}$
4) $\frac{3}{4}$
5) $\frac{1}{3}$
6) $\frac{1}{4}$
7) $\frac{4}{9}$
8) $\frac{1}{2}$
9) $\frac{2}{5}$
10) $\frac{1}{9}$
11) $\frac{5}{9}$
12) $\frac{3}{4}$
13) $\frac{5}{8}$
14) $\frac{13}{16}$
15) $\frac{1}{5}$
16) $\frac{4}{7}$
17) $\frac{1}{2}$
18) $\frac{5}{12}$
19) $\frac{3}{8}$
20) $\frac{1}{4}$
21) $\frac{5}{9}$

Adding and Subtracting Fractions

1) $\frac{7}{6}$
2) $\frac{14}{15}$
3) $\frac{4}{3}$
4) $\frac{83}{36}$
5) $\frac{3}{5}$
6) $\frac{13}{14}$
7) $\frac{23}{20}$
8) $\frac{13}{15}$
9) $\frac{31}{25}$
10) $\frac{2}{5}$
11) $\frac{11}{35}$
12) $\frac{1}{6}$
13) $\frac{13}{45}$
14) $\frac{3}{14}$
15) $\frac{1}{6}$
16) $\frac{1}{36}$
17) $\frac{9}{40}$
18) $\frac{7}{18}$

Multiplying and Dividing Fractions

1) $\frac{2}{15}$
2) $\frac{1}{2}$
3) $\frac{6}{35}$
4) $\frac{1}{8}$
5) $\frac{6}{25}$
6) $\frac{7}{27}$
7) $\frac{1}{4}$
8) $\frac{1}{12}$
9) $\frac{5}{12}$
10) $\frac{8}{9}$
11) $\frac{3}{2}$
12) $\frac{8}{11}$
13) $\frac{55}{7}$
14) $\frac{27}{25}$
15) 1
16) 3
17) $\frac{4}{3}$
18) $\frac{25}{63}$

Adding Mixed Numbers

1) 10
2) $5\frac{1}{2}$
3) $9\frac{3}{5}$
4) 4
5) $10\frac{2}{3}$
6) $4\frac{2}{3}$
7) $3\frac{8}{33}$
8) 4
9) $10\frac{4}{5}$
10) $7\frac{1}{5}$
11) $2\frac{1}{21}$
12) $3\frac{3}{4}$

Subtract Mixed Numbers

1) 1
2) $\frac{1}{4}$
3) $1\frac{2}{5}$
4) $\frac{2}{3}$
5) $\frac{2}{3}$
6) 2
7) $1\frac{19}{33}$
8) 1
9) $4\frac{2}{5}$
10) $6\frac{1}{5}$
11) $1\frac{8}{21}$
12) $\frac{3}{4}$

Multiplying Mixed Numbers

1) $2\frac{1}{12}$
2) $2\frac{2}{3}$
3) $5\frac{10}{21}$
4) $5\frac{31}{40}$

5) $7\frac{17}{25}$
6) $2\frac{2}{9}$
7) $4\frac{1}{16}$
8) $7\frac{12}{25}$

9) $11\frac{1}{3}$
10) $3\frac{9}{10}$
11) $1\frac{2}{3}$
12) $4\frac{2}{25}$

Dividing Mixed Numbers

1) $\frac{22}{25}$
2) $1\frac{19}{20}$
3) $\frac{19}{28}$
4) $\frac{1}{2}$

5) $1\frac{13}{20}$
6) $1\frac{9}{26}$
7) $2\frac{34}{63}$
8) $1\frac{11}{21}$

9) $2\frac{2}{15}$
10) $1\frac{34}{35}$
11) $3\frac{7}{10}$
12) 2

Comparing Decimals

1) 1.25 < 2.3
2) 0.5 > 0.23
3) 3.2 = 3.2
4) 4.58 < 45.8
5) 2.75 > 0.275
6) 5.2 > 5
7) 3.1 > 0.31
8) 6.33 > 0.733
9) 8 > 0.8
10) 4.56 > 0.456
11) 1.12 < 1.14
12) 2.77 < 2.78

13) 6.08 < 6.11
14) 1.11 > 0.211
15) 2.6 > 2.55
16) 1.24 < 1.25
17) 5.52 > 0.552
18) 0.33 > 0.033
19) 14.4 = 14.4
20) 0.05 < 0.50
21) 0.59 < 0.7
22) 0.5 > 0.05
23) 0.90 = 0.9
24) 0.27 < 0.4

Rounding Decimals

1) 0.2
2) 4.0
3) 5.6
4) 0.3
5) 6
6) 0.9
7) 8.2
8) 7
9) 1.63
10) 6.4
11) 2
12) 5
13) 5.9
14) 8.5
15) 81
16) 66
17) 70.8
18) 616
19) 16
20) 96
21) 2
22) 76
23) 116.5
24) 8.1

Adding and Subtracting Decimals

1) 2.96
2) 109.39
3) 94.84
4) 10.73
5) 147.34
6) 22.39
7) 3.5
8) 7.4
9) 6.1
10) 9.5
11) 3.5
12) 7.3

Multiplying and Dividing Decimals

1) 7.2
2) 76.23
3) 3.9
4) 86.33
5) 190.26
6) 22.77
7) 44.46
8) 9820
9) 23990
10) 2.5555...
11) 7.2631...
12) 2.6808...
13) 0.8024...
14) 0.14
15) 0.036
16) 0.424
17) 0.146
18) 0.0018

Converting Between Fractions, Decimals and Mixed Numbers

1) 0.9
2) 0.56
3) 0.75
4) 0.4
5) 0.333...
6) 0.8
7) 1.2
8) 1.6
9) 6.9
10) $\frac{3}{10}$
11) $4\frac{1}{2}$
12) $2\frac{1}{2}$
13) $2\frac{3}{10}$
14) $\frac{4}{5}$
15) $\frac{1}{4}$

16) $\frac{7}{50}$ 18) $\frac{2}{25}$ 20) $2\frac{3}{5}$

17) $\frac{1}{5}$ 19) $\frac{9}{20}$ 21) $5\frac{1}{5}$

Factoring Numbers

1) 1, 2, 4, 17, 34, 68
2) 1, 2, 4, 7, 8, 14, 28, 56
3) 1, 2, 3, 4, 6, 8, 12, 24
4) 1, 2, 4, 5, 8, 10, 20, 40
5) 1, 2, 43, 86
6) 1, 2, 3, 6, 13, 26, 39, 78
7) 1, 2, 5, 10, 25, 50
8) 1, 2, 7, 14, 49, 98
9) 1, 3, 5, 9, 15, 45
10) 1, 2, 13, 26
11) 1, 2, 3, 6, 9, 18, 27, 54
12) 1, 2, 4, 7, 14, 28

13) 1, 5, 11, 55
14) 1, 5, 17, 85
15) 1, 2, 3, 4, 6, 8, 12, 16, 24, 48
16) 2 × 5 × 5
17) 5 × 5
18) 3 × 23
19) 3 × 7
20) 3 × 3 × 5
21) 2 × 2 × 17
22) 2 × 13
23) 2 × 43
24) 3 × 31

Greatest Common Factor

1) 10
2) 2
3) 5
4) 4
5) 1
6) 3
7) 3

8) 2
9) 2
10) 1
11) 2
12) 3
13) 4
14) 10

15) 1
16) 5
17) 2
18) 5
19) 12
20) 2
21) 10

Least Common Multiple

1) 28
2) 15
3) 80
4) 68
5) 24
6) 24
7) 18

8) 30
9) 152
10) 63
11) 551
12) 42
13) 150
14) 8

15) 150
16) 108
17) 72
18) 72
19) 780
20) 120
21) 90

Adding and Subtracting Integers

1) −16	8) 40	15) 32
2) −19	9) −3	16) 56
3) 9	10) −15	17) 12
4) 31	11) −23	18) 13
5) 31	12) 16	19) 53
6) −24	13) −20	20) 42
7) −43	14) 32	

Multiplying and Dividing Integers

1) 16	8) 72	15) −10
2) 18	9) −90	16) 6
3) 120	10) −12	17) 8
4) 72	11) 6	18) −11
5) −132	12) −6	19) 8
6) −50	13) 7	20) 4
7) 64	14) 6	

ACCUPLACER Math in 7 Days

Day 2: Proportions and Variables

Math Topics that you'll learn today:

- Ordering Integers and Numbers
- Arrange, Order, and Comparing Integers
- Order of Operations
- Mixed Integer Computations
- Integers and Absolute Value
- Writing Ratios
- Simplifying Ratios
- Create a Proportion
- Similar Figures
- Simple and Compound Interest
- Ratio and Rates Word Problems
- Percentage Calculations
- Table of Common Percent
- Converting Between Percent, Fractions, and Decimals
- Percent Problems
- Markup, Discount, and Tax
- Expressions and Variables
- Simplifying Variable Expressions
- Simplifying Polynomial Expressions
- Translate Phrases into an Algebraic Statement

"Do not worry about your difficulties in mathematics. I can assure you mine are still greater." – Albert Einstein

ACCUPLACER Math in 7 Days

Ordering Integers and Numbers

Helpful Hints

To compare numbers, you can use number line! As you move from left to right on the number line, you find a bigger number!

Example:

Order integers from least to greatest.

(− 11, − 13, 7, − 2, 12)

− 13 <− 11< − 2 < 7 <12

✎ Order each set of integers from least to greatest.

1) − 15, − 19, 20, − 4, 1   ___, ___, ___, ___, ___, ___

2) 6, − 5, 4, − 3, 2   ___, ___, ___, ___, ___

3) 15, − 42, 19, 0, − 22   ___, ___, ___, ___, ___

4) 26, − 91, 0, − 13, 67, − 55   ___, ___, ___, ___, ___, ___

5) − 17, − 71, 90, − 25, − 54, − 39   ___, ___, ___, ___, ___, ___

6) 98, 5, 46, 19, 77, 24   ___, ___, ___, ___, ___, ___

✎ Order each set of integers from greatest to least.

7) − 2, 5, − 3, 6, − 4   ___, ___, ___, ___, ___

8) − 37, 7, − 17, 27, 47   ___, ___, ___, ___, ___

9) 32, − 27, 19, − 17, 15   ___, ___, ___, ___, ___

10) 68, 81, 21, − 18, 94, 72   ___, ___, ___, ___, ___, ___

www.EffortlessMath.com

Arrange, Order, and Comparing Integers

Helpful Hints

When using a number line, numbers increase as you move to the right.

Examples:

$5 < 7$,

$-5 < -2$

$-18 < -12$

✍ **Arrange these integers in descending order.**

1) 21, 71, − 18, − 10, 82   ___, ___, ___, ___, ___, ___

2) 15, 11, 20, 12, − 9, − 5   ___, ___, ___, ___, ___, ___

3) − 5, 20, 15, 9, −11   ___, ___, ___, ___, ___, ___

4) 19, 18, − 9, − 6, − 11   ___, ___, ___, ___, ___, ___

5) 56, − 34, − 12, − 5, 32   ___, ___, ___, ___, ___, ___

✍ **Compare. Use >, =, <**

6) − 8 ____ 12   11) − 56 ____ − 58

7) − 10 ____ −16   12) 78 ____ 87

8) 43 ____ 34   13) − 92 ____ − 102

9) 15 ____ −16   14) − 12 ____ − 12

10) − 354 ____ −345   15) − 721 ____ − 821

Order of Operations

Helpful Hints
- Use "order of operations" rule when there are more than one math operation.
- PEMDAS
(parentheses / exponents / multiply / divide / add / subtract)

Example:

$(12 + 4) \div (-4) = -4$

✏️ *Evaluate each expression.*

1) $(2 \times 2) + 5$

2) $24 - (3 \times 3)$

3) $(6 \times 4) + 8$

4) $25 - (4 \times 2)$

5) $(6 \times 5) + 3$

6) $64 - (2 \times 4)$

7) $25 + (1 \times 8)$

8) $(6 \times 7) + 7$

9) $48 \div (4 + 4)$

10) $(7 + 11) \div (-2)$

11) $9 + (2 \times 5) + 10$

12) $(5 + 8) \times \frac{3}{5} + 2$

13) $2 \times 7 - (\frac{10}{9-4})$

14) $(12 + 2 - 5) \times 7 - 1$

15) $(\frac{7}{5-1}) \times (2 + 6) \times 2$

16) $20 \div (4 - (10 - 8))$

17) $\frac{50}{4(5-4)-3}$

18) $2 + (8 \times 2)$

38

Mixed Integer Computations

Helpful Hints

It worth remembering:

(negative) × (negative) = positive

(negative) ÷ (negative) = positive

(negative) × (positive) = negative

(negative) ÷ (positive) = negative

(positive) × (positive) = positive

Example:

$(-5) + 6 = 1$

$(-3) \times (-2) = 6$

$(9) \div (-3) = -3$

✎ Compute.

1) $(-70) \div (-5)$

2) $(-14) \times 3$

3) $(-4) \times (-15)$

4) $(-65) \div 5$

5) $18 \times (-7)$

6) $(-12) \times (-2)$

7) $\dfrac{(-60)}{(-20)}$

8) $24 \div (-8)$

9) $22 \div (-11)$

10) $\dfrac{(-27)}{3}$

11) $4 \times (-4)$

12) $\dfrac{(-48)}{12}$

13) $(-14) \times (-2)$

14) $(-7) \times (7)$

15) $\dfrac{-30}{-6}$

16) $(-54) \div 6$

17) $(-60) \div (-5)$

18) $(-7) \times (-12)$

19) $(-14) \times 5$

20) $88 \div (-8)$

Integers and Absolute Value

Helpful Hints

To find an absolute value of a number, just find it's distance from 0!

Example:

|−6| = 6

|6| = 6

|−12| = 12

|12| = 12

✎ Write absolute value of each number.

1) − 4

2) − 7

3) − 8

4) 4

5) 5

6) − 10

7) 1

8) 6

9) 8

10) − 2

11) − 1

12) 10

13) 3

14) 7

15) − 5

16) − 3

17) − 9

18) 2

19) 4

20) − 6

21) 9

✎ Evaluate.

22) |−43| − |12| + 10

23) 76 + |−15 − 45| − |3|

24) 30 + |−62| − 46

25) |32| − |−78| + 90

26) |−35 + 4| + 6 − 4

27) |−4| + |−11|

28) |−6 + 3 − 4| + |7 + 7|

29) |−9| + |−19| − 5

Writing Ratios

Helpful Hints — A ratio is a comparison of two numbers. Ratio can be written as a division.

Example:

$3 : 5$, or $\frac{3}{5}$

✎ *Express each ratio as a rate and unite rate.*

1) 120 miles on 4 gallons of gas.

2) 24 dollars for 6 books.

3) 200 miles on 14 gallons of gas

4) 24 inches of snow in 8 hours

✎ *Express each ratio as a fraction in the simplest form.*

5) 3 feet out of 30 feet

6) 18 cakes out of 42 cakes

7) 16 dimes t0 24 dimes

8) 12 dimes out of 48 coins

9) 14 cups to 84 cups

10) 45 gallons to 65 gallons

11) 10 miles out of 40 miles

12) 22 blue cars out of 55 cars

13) 32 pennies to 300 pennies

14) 24 beetles out of 86 insects

Simplifying Ratios

Helpful Hints

— You can calculate equivalent ratios by multiplying or dividing both sides of the ratio by the same number.

Examples:

3 : 6 = 1 : 2

4 : 9 = 8 : 18

Reduce each ratio.

1) 21 : 49

2) 20 : 40

3) 10 : 50

4) 14 : 18

5) 45 : 27

6) 49 : 21

7) 100 : 10

8) 12 : 8

9) 35 : 45

10) 8 : 20

11) 25 : 35

12) 21 : 27

13) 52 : 82

14) 12 : 36

15) 24 : 3

16) 15 : 30

17) 3 : 36

18) 8 : 16

19) 6 : 100

20) 2 : 20

21) 10 : 60

22) 14 : 63

23) 68 : 80

24) 8 : 80

Create a Proportion

Helpful Hints

— A proportion contains 2 equal fractions! A proportion simply means that two fractions are equal.

Example:

2, 4, 8, 16

$$\frac{2}{4} = \frac{8}{16}$$

✎ Create proportion from the given set of numbers.

1) 1, 6, 2, 3

2) 12, 144, 1, 12

3) 16, 4, 8, 2

4) 9, 5, 27, 15

5) 7, 10, 60, 42

6) 8, 7, 24, 21

7) 10, 5, 8, 4

8) 3, 12, 8, 2

9) 2, 2, 1, 4

10) 3, 6, 7, 14

11) 2, 6, 5, 15

12) 7, 2, 14, 4

Similar Figures

Helpful Hints

– Two or more figures are similar if the corresponding angles are equal, and the corresponding sides are in proportion.

Example:

3–4–5 triangle is similar to a

6–8–10 triangle

✎ *Each pair of figures is similar. Find the missing side.*

1)

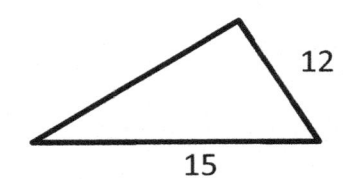

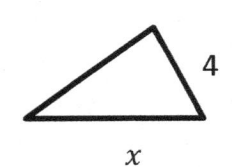

12, 15, 4, x

2)

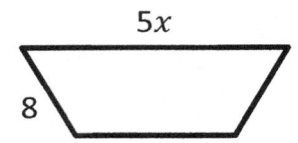

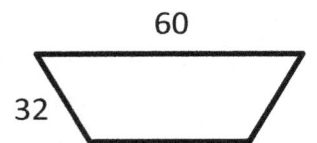

$5x$, 8, 60, 32

3)

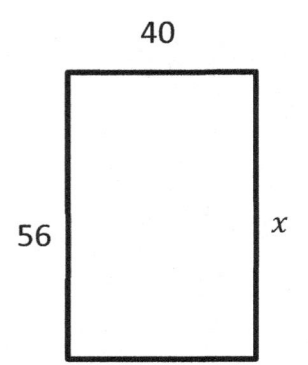

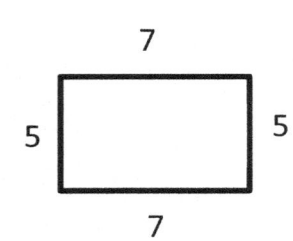

40, 56, x, 7, 5, 5, 7

44 www.EffortlessMath.com

Simple Interest

Helpful Hints

Simple Interest: The charge for borrowing money or the return for lending it.
Interest = principal × rate × time

$$I = prt$$

Example:

$450 at 7% for 8 years.

$$I = prt$$

$$I = 450 \times 0.07 \times 8 = \$252 =$$

✎ **Use simple interest to find the ending balance.**

1) $1,300 at 5% for 6 years.

2) $5,400 at 7.5% for 6 months.

3) $25,600 at 9.2% for 5 years

4) $24,000 at 8.5% for 9 years.

5) $450 at 7% for 8 years.

6) $54,200 at 8% for 5 years.

7) $240 interest is earned on a principal of $1500 at a simple interest rate of 4% interest per year. For how many years was the principal invested?

8) A new car, valued at $28,000, depreciates at 9% per year from original price. Find the value of the car 3 years after purchase.

9) Sara puts $2,000 into an investment yielding 5% annual simple interest; she left the money in for five years. How much interest does Sara get at the end of those five years?

Ratio and Rates Word Problems

Helpful Hints

To solve a ratio or a rate word problem, create a proportion and use cross multiplication method!

Example:

$$\frac{x}{4} = \frac{8}{16}$$

$$16x = 4 \times 8$$

$$x = 2$$

✎ Solve.

1) In a party, 10 soft drinks are required for every 12 guests. If there are 252 guests, how many soft drink is required?

2) In Jack's class, 18 of the students are tall and 10 are short. In Michael's class 54 students are tall and 30 students are short. Which class has a higher ratio of tall to short students?

3) Are these ratios equivalent?
12 cards to 72 animals   11 marbles to 66 marbles

4) The price of 3 apples at the Quick Market is $1.44. The price of 5 of the same apples at Walmart is $2.50. Which place is the better buy?

5) The bakers at a Bakery can make 160 bagels in 4 hours. How many bagels can they bake in 16 hours? What is that rate per hour?

6) You can buy 5 cans of green beans at a supermarket for $3.40. How much does it cost to buy 35 cans of green beans?

Percentage Calculations

Helpful Hints — Use the following formula to find part, whole, or percent:

$$\text{part} = \frac{\text{percent}}{100} \times \text{whole}$$

Example:

$$\frac{20}{100} \times 100 = 20$$

✎ **Calculate the percentages.**

1) 50% of 25
2) 80% of 15
3) 30% of 34
4) 70% of 45
5) 10% of 0
6) 80% of 22
7) 65% of 8
8) 78% of 54
9) 50% of 80
10) 20% of 10
11) 40% of 40
12) 90% of 0
13) 20% of 70
14) 55% of 60
15) 80% of 10
16) 20% of 880
17) 70% of 100
18) 80% of 90

✎ **Solve.**

19) 50 is what percentage of 75?

20) What percentage of 100 is 70

21) Find what percentage of 60 is 35.

22) 40 is what percentage of 80?

Converting Between Percent, Fractions, and Decimals

Helpful Hints

− To a percent: Move the decimal point 2 places to the right and add the % symbol.

− Divide by 100 to convert a number from percent to decimal.

Examples:

30% = 0.3

0.24 = 24%

✎ *Converting fractions to decimals.*

1) $\dfrac{50}{100}$ 4) $\dfrac{80}{100}$ 7) $\dfrac{90}{100}$

2) $\dfrac{38}{100}$ 5) $\dfrac{7}{100}$ 8) $\dfrac{20}{100}$

3) $\dfrac{15}{100}$ 6) $\dfrac{35}{100}$ 9) $\dfrac{7}{100}$

✎ *Write each decimal as a percent.*

10) 0.5   13) 0.524   16) 3.63

11) 0.9   14) 0.1   17) 0.008

12) 0.002   15) 0.03   18) 4.78

Percent Problems

Helpful Hints

Base = Part ÷ Percent
Part = Percent × Base
Percent = Part ÷ Base

Example:

2 is 10% of 20.

2 ÷ 0.10 = 20

2 = 0.10 × 20

0.10 = 2 ÷ 20

✍ Solve each problem.

1) 51 is 340% of what?

2) 93% of what number is 97?

3) 27% of 142 is what number?

4) What percent of 125 is 29.3?

5) 60 is what percent of 126?

6) 67 is 67% of what?

7) 67 is 13% of what?

8) 41% of 78 is what?

9) 1 is what percent of 52.6?

10) What is 59% of 14 m?

11) What is 90% of 130 inches?

12) 16 inches is 35% of what?

13) 90% of 54.4 hours is what?

14) What percent of 33.5 is 21?

15) Liam scored 22 out of 30 marks in Algebra, 35 out of 40 marks in science and 89 out of 100 marks in mathematics. In which subject his percentage of marks in best?

16) Ella require 50% to pass. If she gets 280 marks and falls short by 20 marks, what were the maximum marks she could have got?

Markup, Discount, and Tax

Helpful Hints

- **Markup** = selling price − cost
  Markup rate = markup divided by the cost

- **Discount:**
  Multiply the regular price by the rate of discount

  Selling price =

  original price − discount

- **Tax:**
  To find tax, multiply the tax rate to the taxable amount (income, property value, etc.)

Example:

Original price of a microphone: $49.99, discount: 5%, tax: 5%

Selling price = 49.87

Find the selling price of each item.

1) Cost of a pen: $1.95, markup: 70%, discount: 40%, tax: 5%

2) Cost of a puppy: $349.99, markup: 41%, discount: 23%

3) Cost of a shirt: $14.95, markup: 25%, discount: 45%

4) Cost of an oil change: $21.95, markup: 95%

5) Cost of computer: $1,850.00, markup: 75%

Expressions and Variables

Helpful Hints

A variable is a letter that represents unknown numbers. A variable can be used in the same manner as all other numbers:

Addition	$2 + a$	2 plus a
Subtraction	$y - 3$	y minus 3
Division	$\dfrac{4}{x}$	4 divided by x
Multiplication	$5a$	5 times a

✎ **Simplify each expression.**

1) $x + 5x$,
   use $x = 5$

2) $8(-3x + 9) + 6$,
   use $x = 6$

3) $10x - 2x + 6 - 5$,
   use $x = 5$

4) $2x - 3x - 9$,
   use $x = 7$

5) $(-6)(-2x - 4y)$,
   use $x = 1, y = 3$

6) $8x + 2 + 4y$,
   use $x = 9, y = 2$

7) $(-6)(-8x - 9y)$,
   use $x = 5, y = 5$

8) $6x + 5y$,
   use $x = 7, y = 4$

✎ **Simplify each expression.**

9) $5(-4 + 2x)$

10) $-3 - 5x - 6x + 9$

11) $6x - 3x - 8 + 10$

12) $(-8)(6x - 4) + 12$

13) $9(7x + 4) + 6x$

14) $(-9)(-5x + 2)$

Simplifying Variable Expressions

Helpful Hints

– Combine "like" terms. (values with same variable and same power)

– Use distributive property if necessary.

Distributive Property:

$a(b + c) = ab + ac$

Example:

$2x + 2(1 - 5x) =$

$2x + 2 - 10x = -8x + 2$

✍ *Simplify each expression.*

1) $-2 - x^2 - 6x^2$

2) $3 + 10x^2 + 2$

3) $8x^2 + 6x + 7x^2$

4) $5x^2 - 12x^2 + 8x$

5) $2x^2 - 2x - x$

6) $(-6)(8x - 4)$

7) $4x + 6(2 - 5x)$

8) $10x + 8(10x - 6)$

9) $9(-2x - 6) - 5$

10) $3(x + 9)$

11) $7x + 3 - 3x$

12) $2.5x^2 \times (-8x)$

✍ *Simplify.*

13) $-2(4 - 6x) - 3x$, $x = 1$

14) $2x + 8x$, $x = 2$

15) $9 - 2x + 5x + 2$, $x = 5$

16) $5(3x + 7)$, $x = 3$

17) $2(3 - 2x) - 4$, $x = 6$

18) $5x + 3x - 8$, $x = 3$

19) $x - 7x$, $x = 8$

20) $5(-2 - 9x)$, $x = 4$

Simplifying Polynomial Expressions

Helpful Hints

- In mathematics, a polynomial is an expression consisting of variables and coefficients that involves only the operations of addition, subtraction, multiplication, and non–negative integer exponents of variables.

$P(x) = a_0 x^n + a_1 x^{n-1} + \ldots + a_{n-2} 2x^2 + a_{n-1} x + a_n$

Example:

An example of a polynomial of a single indeterminate x is

$x^2 - 4x + 7$.

An example for three variables is

$x^3 + 2xyz^2 - yz + 1$

✍ *Simplify each polynomial.*

1) $4x^5 - 5x^6 + 15x^5 - 12x^6 + 3x^6$

2) $(-3x^5 + 12 - 4x) + (8x^4 + 5x + 5x^5)$

3) $10x^2 - 5x^4 + 14x^3 - 20x^4 + 15x^3 - 8x^4$

4) $-6x^2 + 5x^2 - 7x^3 + 12 + 22$

5) $12x^5 - 5x^3 + 8x^2 - 8x^5$

6) $5x^3 + 1 + x^2 - 2x - 10x$

7) $14x^2 - 6x^3 - 2x(4x^2 + 2x)$

8) $(4x^4 - 2x) - (4x - 2x^4)$

9) $(3x^2 + 1) - (4 + 2x^2)$

10) $(2x + 2) - (7x + 6)$

11) $(12x^3 + 4x^4) - (2x^4 - 6x^3)$

12) $(12 + 3x^3) + (6x^3 + 6)$

13) $(5x^2 - 3) + (2x^2 - 3x^3)$

14) $(23x^3 - 12x^2) - (2x^2 - 9x^3)$

15) $(4x - 3x^3) - (3x^3 + 4x)$

Translate Phrases into an Algebraic Statement

Helpful Hints

Translating key words and phrases into algebraic expressions:

Addition: plus, more than, the sum of, etc.

Subtraction: minus, less than, decreased, etc.

Multiplication: times, product, multiplied, etc.

Division: quotient, divided, ratio, etc.

Example:

eight more than a number is 20

$8 + x = 20$

✎ *Write an algebraic expression for each phrase.*

1) A number increased by forty–two.

2) The sum of fifteen and a number

3) The difference between fifty–six and a number.

4) The quotient of thirty and a number.

5) Twice a number decreased by 25.

6) Four times the sum of a number and − 12.

7) A number divided by − 20.

8) The quotient of 60 and the product of a number and − 5.

9) Ten subtracted from a number.

10) The difference of six and a number.

Answers of Worksheets – Day 3

Ordering Integers and Numbers

1) −19, −15, −4, 1, 20
2) −5, −3, 2, 4, 6
3) −42, −22, 0, 15, 19
4) −91, −55, −13, 0, 26, 67
5) −71, −54, −39, −25, −17, 90
6) 5, 19, 24, 46, 77, 98
7) 6, 5, −2, −3, −4
8) 47, 27, 7, −17, −37
9) 32, 19, 15, −17, −27
10) 94, 81, 72, 68, 21, −18

Arrange and Order, Comparing Integers

1) 82, 71, 21, −10, −18
2) 20, 15, 12, 11, −5, −9
3) 20, 15, 9, −5, −11
4) 19, 18, −6, −9, −11
5) 56, 32, −5, −12, −34
6) <
7) >
8) >
9) >
10) <
11) >
12) <
13) >
14) =
15) >

Order of Operations

1) 9
2) 15
3) 32
4) 17
5) 33
6) 56
7) 33
8) 49
9) 6
10) −9
11) 29
12) 9.8
13) 12
14) 62
15) 28
16) 10
17) 50
18) 18

Mixed Integer Computations

1) 14
2) −42
3) 60
4) −13
5) −126
6) 24
7) 3
8) −3
9) −2
10) −9
11) −16
12) −4
13) 28
14) −49
15) 5
16) −9
17) 12
18) 84
19) −70
20) −11

Integers and Absolute Value

1) 4
2) 7
3) 8
4) 4
5) 5
6) 10
7) 1
8) 6
9) 8
10) 2
11) 1
12) 10
13) 3
14) 7
15) 5
16) 3
17) 9
18) 2
19) 4
20) 6
21) 9
22) 41
23) 133
24) 46
25) 44
26) 33
27) 15
28) 21
29) 23

Writing Ratios

1) $\frac{120\ miles}{4\ gallons}$, 30 miles per gallon

2) $\frac{24\ dollars}{6\ books}$, 4.00 dollars per book

3) $\frac{200\ miles}{14\ gallons}$, 14.29 miles per gallon

4) $\frac{24"\ of\ snow}{8\ hours}$, 3 inches of snow per hour

5) $\frac{1}{10}$
6) $\frac{3}{7}$
7) $\frac{2}{3}$
8) $\frac{1}{4}$
9) $\frac{1}{6}$
10) $\frac{9}{13}$
11) $\frac{1}{4}$
12) $\frac{2}{5}$
13) $\frac{8}{75}$
14) $\frac{12}{43}$

Simplifying Ratios

1) 3 : 7
2) 1 : 2
3) 1 : 5
4) 7 : 9
5) 5 : 3
6) 7 : 3
7) 10 : 1
8) 3 : 2
9) 7 : 9
10) 2 : 5
11) 5 : 7
12) 7 : 9
13) 26 : 41
14) 1 : 3
15) 8 : 1
16) 1 : 2
17) 1 : 12
18) 1 : 2
19) 3 : 50
20) 1 : 10
21) 1 : 6
22) 2 : 9
23) 17 : 20
24) 1 : 10

Create a Proportion

1) 1 : 3 = 2 : 6
2) 12 : 144 = 1 : 12
3) 2 : 4 = 8 : 16
4) 5 : 15 = 9 : 27
5) 7 : 42, 10 : 60
6) 7 : 21 = 8 : 24
7) 8 : 10 = 4 : 5
8) 2 : 3 = 8 : 12
9) 4 : 2 = 2 : 1
10) 7 : 3 = 14 : 6
11) 5 : 2 = 15 : 6
12) 7 : 2 = 14 : 4

Similar Figures

1) 5
2) 3
3) 56

Simple Interest

1) $1,690.00
2) $5,602.50
3) $37,376.00
4) $42,360.00
5) $702.00
6) $75,880.00
7) 4 years
8) $20,440
9) $500

Ratio and Rates Word Problems

1) 210
2) The ratio for both class is equal to 9 to 5.
3) Yes! Both ratios are 1 to 6
4) The price at the Quick Market is a better buy.
5) 640, the rate is 40 per hour.
6) $23.80

Percentage Calculations

1) 12.5
2) 12
3) 10.2
4) 31.5
5) 0
6) 17.6
7) 5.2
8) 42.12
9) 40
10) 2
11) 16
12) 0
13) 14
14) 33
15) 8
16) 176
17) 70
18) 72
19) 67%
20) 70%
21) 58%
22) 50%

Converting Between Percent, Fractions, and Decimals

1) 0.5
2) 0.38
3) 0.15
4) 0.8
5) 0.07
6) 0.35
7) 0.9
8) 0.2
9) 0.07
10) 50%
11) 90%
12) 0.2%
13) 52.4%
14) 10%
15) 3%
16) 363%
17) 0.8%
18) 478%

Percent Problems

1) 15
2) 104.3
3) 38.34
4) 23.44%
5) 47.6%
6) 100
7) 515.4
8) 31.98
9) 1.9%
10) 8.3 m
11) 117 inches
12) 45.7 inches
13) 49 hours
14) 62.7%
15) Mathematics
16) 600

Markup, Discount, and Tax

1) $2.09
2) $379.98
3) $10.28
4) $36.22
5) $3,237.50

Expressions and Variables

1) 30
2) –66
3) 41
4) –16
5) 84
6) 82
7) 510
8) 62
9) 10x – 20
10) 6 – 11x
11) 3x + 2
12) 44 – 48x
13) 69x + 36
14) 45x – 18

Simplifying Variable Expressions

1) $-7x^2 - 2$
2) $10x^2 + 5$
3) $15x^2 + 6x$
4) $-7x^2 + 8x$
5) $2x^2 - 3x$
6) $-48x + 24$
7) $-26x + 12$
8) $90x - 48$
9) $-18x - 59$
10) $3x + 27$
11) $4x + 3$
12) $-20x^3$
13) 1
14) 20
15) 26
16) 80
17) –22
18) 16
19) –48
20) –190

Simplifying Polynomial Expressions

1) $-14x^6 + 19x^5$
2) $2x^5 + 8x^4 + x + 12$
3) $-33x^4 + 29x^3 + 10x^2$
4) $-7x^3 - x^2 + 34$
5) $4x^5 - 5x^3 + 8x^2$
6) $5x^3 + x^2 - 12x + 1$
7) $-14x^3 + 10x^2$
8) $6x^4 - 6x$
9) $x^2 - 3$
10) $-5x - 4$
11) $2x^4 + 18x^3$
12) $9x^3 + 18$
13) $-3x^3 + 7x^2 - 3$
14) $32x^3 - 14x^2$
15) $-6x^3$

Translate Phrases into an Algebraic Statement

1) X + 42
2) 15 + x
3) 56 – x
4) 30/x
5) 2x – 25
6) $4(x + (-12))$
7) $\dfrac{x}{-20}$
8) $\dfrac{60}{-5x}$
9) x – 10
10) 6 – x

Day 3: Equations and Inequalities

Math Topics that you'll learn today:

- ✓ The Distributive Property
- ✓ Evaluating One Variable
- ✓ Evaluating Two Variables
- ✓ Combining like Terms
- ✓ One–Step Equations
- ✓ Two–Step Equations
- ✓ Multi–Step Equations
- ✓ Graphing Single –Variable Inequalities
- ✓ One–Step Inequalities
- ✓ Two–Step Inequalities
- ✓ Multi–Step Inequalities
- ✓ Finding Slope
- ✓ Graphing Lines Using Slope–Intercept Form
- ✓ Graphing Lines Using Standard Form

Without mathematics, there's nothing you can do. Everything around you is mathematics. Everything around you is numbers." – Shakuntala Devi

The Distributive Property

Helpful Hints

Distributive Property:

$a(b + c) = ab + ac$

Example:

$3(4 + 3x)$

$= 12 + 9x$

✍ Use the distributive property to simply each expression.

1) $-(-2 - 5x)$

2) $(-6x + 2)(-1)$

3) $(-5)(x - 2)$

4) $-(7 - 3x)$

5) $8(8 + 2x)$

6) $2(12 + 2x)$

7) $(-6x + 8)\,4$

8) $(3 - 6x)(-7)$

9) $(-12)(2x + 1)$

10) $(8 - 2x)\,9$

11) $(-2x)(-1 + 9x) - 4x(4 + 5x)$

12) $3(-5x - 3) + 4(6 - 3x)$

13) $(-2)(x + 4) - (2 + 3x)$

14) $(-4)(3x - 2) + 6(x + 1)$

15) $(-5)(4x - 1) + 4(x + 2)$

16) $(-3)(x + 4) - (2 + 3x)$

Evaluating One Variable

Helpful Hints

— To evaluate one variable expression, find the variable and substitute a number for that variable.

— Perform the arithmetic operations.

Example:

$4x + 8, x = 6$

$4(6) + 8 = 24 + 8 = 32$

✎ **Simplify each algebraic expression.**

1) $9 - x$, $x = 3$

2) $x + 2$, $x = 5$

3) $3x + 7$, $x = 6$

4) $x + (-5)$, $x = -2$

5) $3x + 6$, $x = 4$

6) $4x + 6$, $x = -1$

7) $10 + 2x - 6$, $x = 3$

8) $10 - 3x$, $x = 8$

9) $\frac{20}{x} - 3$, $x = 5$

10) $(-3) + \frac{x}{4} + 2x$, $x = 16$

11) $(-2) + \frac{x}{7}$, $x = 21$

12) $(-\frac{14}{x}) - 9 + 4x$, $x = 2$

13) $(-\frac{6}{x}) - 9 + 2x$, $x = 3$

14) $(-2) + \frac{x}{8}$, $x = 16$

15) $8(5x - 12)$, $x = -2$

Evaluating Two Variables

Helpful Hints

To evaluate an algebraic expression, substitute a number for each variable and perform the arithmetic operations.

Example:

$2x + 4y - 3 + 2,$

$x = 5, y = 3$

$2(5) + 4(3) - 3 + 2$
$= 10$
$+ 12 - 3 + 2$
$= 21$

✍ Simplify each algebraic expression.

1) $2x + 4y - 3 + 2,$
   $x = 5, y = 3$

2) $(-\frac{12}{x}) + 1 + 5y,$
   $x = 6, y = 8$

3) $(-4)(-2a - 2b),$
   $a = 5, b = 3$

4) $10 + 3x + 7 - 2y,$
   $x = 7, y = 6$

5) $9x + 2 - 4y,$
   $x = 7, y = 5$

6) $6 + 3(-2x - 3y),$
   $x = 9, y = 7$

7) $12x + y,$
   $x = 4, y = 8$

8) $x \times 4 \div y,$
   $x = 3, y = 2$

9) $2x + 14 + 4y,$
   $x = 6, y = 8$

10) $4a - (5 - b),$
    $a = 4, b = 6$

Combining like Terms

Helpful Hints

— Terms are separated by "+" and "–" signs.

— Like terms are terms with same variables and same powers.

— Be sure to use the "+" or "–" that is in front of the coefficient.

Example:

$22x + 6 + 2x =$

$24x + 6$

✎ Simplify each expression.

1) $5 + 2x - 8$

2) $(-2x + 6)\,2$

3) $7 + 3x + 6x - 4$

4) $(-4) - (3)(5x + 8)$

5) $9x - 7x - 5$

6) $x - 12x$

7) $7(3x + 6) + 2x$

8) $(-11x) - 10x$

9) $3x - 12 - 5x$

10) $13 + 4x - 5$

11) $(-22x) + 8x$

12) $2(4 + 3x) - 7x$

13) $(-4x) - (6 - 14x)$

14) $5(6x - 1) + 12x$

15) $22x + 6 + 2x$

16) $(-13x) - 14x$

17) $(-6x) - 9 + 15x$

18) $(-6x) + 7x$

19) $(-5x) + 12 + 7x$

20) $(-3x) - 9 + 15x$

21) $20x - 19x$

One–Step Equations

Helpful Hints

- The values of two expressions on both sides of an equation are equal.
$$ax + b = c$$

- You only need to perform one Math operation in order to solve the equation.

Example:

$-8x = 16$

$x = -2$

✎ Solve each equation.

1) x + 3 = 17

2) 22 = (− 8) + x

3) 3x = (− 30)

4) (− 36) = (− 6x)

5) (− 6) = 4 + x

6) 2 + x = (− 2)

7) 20x = (− 220)

8) 18 = x + 5

9) (− 23) + x = (− 19)

10) 5x = (− 45)

11) x − 12 = (− 25)

12) x − 3 = (− 12)

13) (− 35) = x − 27

14) 8 = 2x

15) (− 6x) = 36

16) (− 55) = (− 5x)

17) x − 30 = 20

18) 8x = 32

19) 36 = (− 4x)

20) 4x = 68

21) 30x = 300

Two–Step Equations

Helpful Hints
- You only need to perform two math operations (add, subtract, multiply, or divide) to solve the equation.
- Simplify using the inverse of addition or subtraction.
- Simplify further by using the inverse of multiplication or division.

Example:
$-2(x-1) = 42$
$(x-1) = -21$
$x = -20$

✎ Solve each equation.

1) $5(8 + x) = 20$

2) $(-7)(x - 9) = 42$

3) $(-12)(2x - 3) = (-12)$

4) $6(1 + x) = 12$

5) $12(2x + 4) = 60$

6) $7(3x + 2) = 42$

7) $8(14 + 2x) = (-34)$

8) $(-15)(2x - 4) = 48$

9) $3(x + 5) = 12$

10) $\dfrac{3x - 12}{6} = 4$

11) $(-12) = \dfrac{x + 15}{6}$

12) $110 = (-5)(2x - 6)$

13) $\dfrac{x}{8} - 12 = 4$

14) $20 = 12 + \dfrac{x}{4}$

15) $\dfrac{-24 + x}{6} = (-12)$

16) $(-4)(5 + 2x) = (-100)$

17) $(-12x) + 20 = 32$

18) $\dfrac{-2 + 6x}{4} = (-8)$

19) $\dfrac{x + 6}{5} = (-5)$

20) $(-9) + \dfrac{x}{4} = (-15)$

Multi–Step Equations

Helpful Hints

– Combine "like" terms on one side.

– Bring variables to one side by adding or subtracting.

– Simplify using the inverse of addition or subtraction.

– Simplify further by using the inverse of multiplication or division.

Example:

$3x + 15 = -2x + 5$

Add 2x both sides

$5x + 15 = +5$

Subtract 15 both sides

$5x = -10$

Divide by 5 both sides

$x = -2$

✎ **Solve each equation.**

1) $-(2 - 2x) = 10$

2) $-12 = -(2x + 8)$

3) $3x + 15 = (-2x) + 5$

4) $-28 = (-2x) - 12x$

5) $2(1 + 2x) + 2x = -118$

6) $3x - 18 = 22 + x - 3 + x$

7) $12 - 2x = (-32) - x + x$

8) $7 - 3x - 3x = 3 - 3x$

9) $6 + 10x + 3x = (-30) + 4x$

10) $(-3x) - 8(-1 + 5x) = 352$

11) $24 = (-4x) - 8 + 8$

12) $9 = 2x - 7 + 6x$

13) $6(1 + 6x) = 294$

14) $-10 = (-4x) - 6x$

15) $4x - 2 = (-7) + 5x$

16) $5x - 14 = 8x + 4$

17) $40 = -(4x - 8)$

18) $(-18) - 6x = 6(1 + 3x)$

19) $x - 5 = -2(6 + 3x)$

20) $6 = 1 - 2x + 5$

Graphing Single–Variable Inequalities

Helpful Hints
— Isolate the variable.
— Find the value of the inequality on the number line.
— For less than or greater than draw open circle on the value of the variable.
— If there is an equal sign too, then use filled circle.
— Draw a line to the right direction.

✎ Draw a graph for each inequality.

1) $-2 > x$

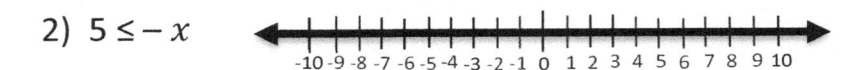

2) $5 \leq -x$

3) $x > 7$

4) $-x > 1.5$

One–Step Inequalities

Helpful Hints

– Isolate the variable.

– For dividing both sides by negative numbers, flip the direction of the inequality sign.

Example:

$x + 4 \geq 11$

$x \geq 7$

✎ **Solve each inequality and graph it.**

1) $x + 9 \geq 11$

2) $x - 4 \leq 2$

3) $6x \geq 36$

4) $7 + x < 16$

5) $x + 8 \leq 1$

6) $3x > 12$

7) $3x < 24$

Two–Step Inequalities

Helpful Hints

– Isolate the variable.

– For dividing both sides by negative numbers, flip the direction of the of the inequality sign.

– Simplify using the inverse of addition or subtraction.

– Simplify further by using the inverse of multiplication or division.

Example:

$2x + 9 \geq 11$

$2x \geq 2$

$x \geq 1$

✎ Solve each inequality and graph it.

1) $3x - 4 \leq 5$

2) $2x - 2 \leq 6$

3) $4x - 4 \leq 8$

4) $3x + 6 \geq 12$

5) $6x - 5 \geq 19$

6) $2x - 4 \leq 6$

7) $8x - 4 \leq 4$

8) $6x + 4 \leq 10$

9) $5x + 4 \leq 9$

10) $7x - 4 \leq 3$

11) $4x - 19 < 19$

12) $2x - 3 < 21$

13) $7 + 4x \geq 19$

14) $9 + 4x < 21$

15) $3 + 2x \geq 19$

16) $6 + 4x < 22$

Multi–Step Inequalities

Helpful Hints

− Isolate the variable.

− Simplify using the inverse of addition or subtraction.

− Simplify further by using the inverse of multiplication or division.

Example:

$\dfrac{7x + 1}{3} \geq 5$

$7x + 1 \geq 15$

$7x \geq 14$

$x \geq 7$

✎ Solve each inequality.

1) $\dfrac{9x}{7} - 7 < 2$

2) $\dfrac{4x + 8}{2} \leq 12$

3) $\dfrac{3x - 8}{7} > 1$

4) $-3(x - 7) > 21$

5) $4 + \dfrac{x}{3} < 7$

6) $\dfrac{2x + 6}{4} \leq 10$

Finding Slope

Helpful Hints

Slope of a line:

$$\frac{y_2 - y_1}{x_2 - x_1} = \frac{\text{rise}}{\text{run}}$$

Example:

(2, −10), (3, 6)

slope = 16

✏️ **Find the slope of the line through each pair of points.**

1) (1, 1), (3, 5)

2) (4, − 6), (− 3, − 8)

3) (7, − 12), (5, 10)

4) (19, 3), (20, 3)

5) (15, 8), (− 17, 9)

6) (6, − 12), (15, − 3)

7) (3, 1), (7, − 5)

8) (3, − 2), (− 7, 8)

9) (15, − 3), (− 9, 5)

10) (− 4, 7), (− 6, − 4)

11) (6, − 8), (− 11, − 7)

12) (− 6, 13), (17, − 9)

13) (− 10, − 2), (− 6, − 5)

14) (4, 5), (− 4, 10)

15) (− 3, 1), (− 17, 2)

16) (7, 0), (− 13, − 11)

17) (17, − 13), (17, 8)

18) (12, 2), (− 7, 5)

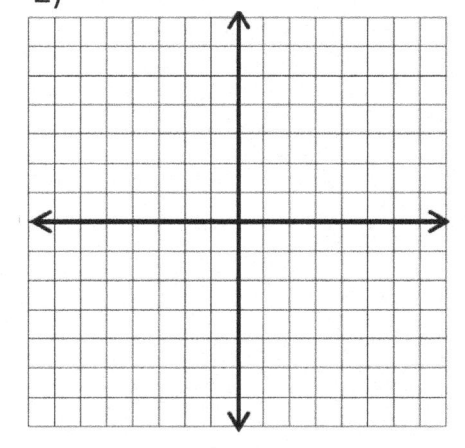

Graphing Lines Using Slope–Intercept Form

Helpful Hints

Slope–intercept form: given the slope m and the y–intercept b, then the equation of the line is:

$y = mx + b$.

Example:

$y = 8x - 3$

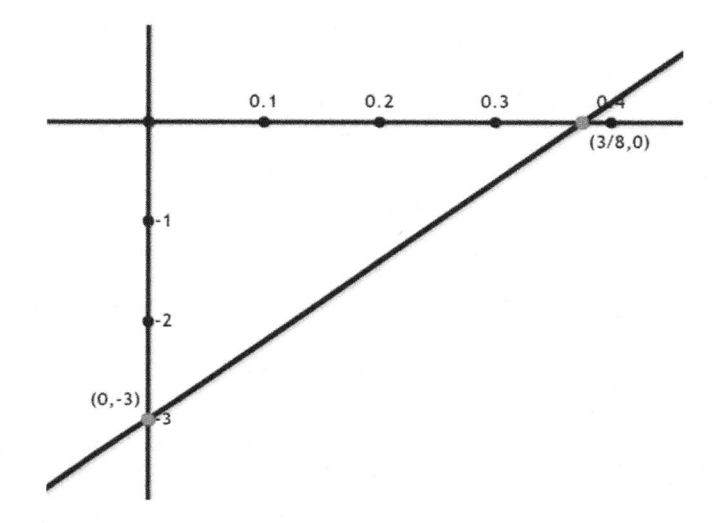

Sketch the graph of each line.

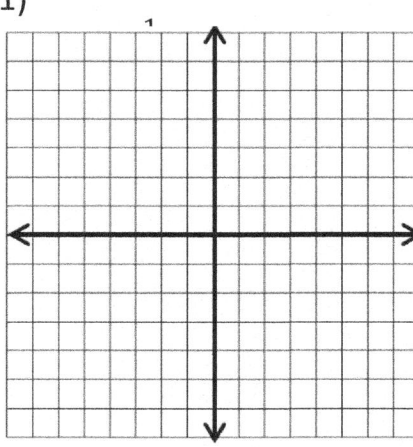

1)

2)

Graphing Lines Using Standard Form

Helpful Hints
– Find the –intercept of the line by putting zero for y.
– Find the y–intercept of the line by putting zero for the x.
– Connect these two points.

Example:

$x + 4y = 12$

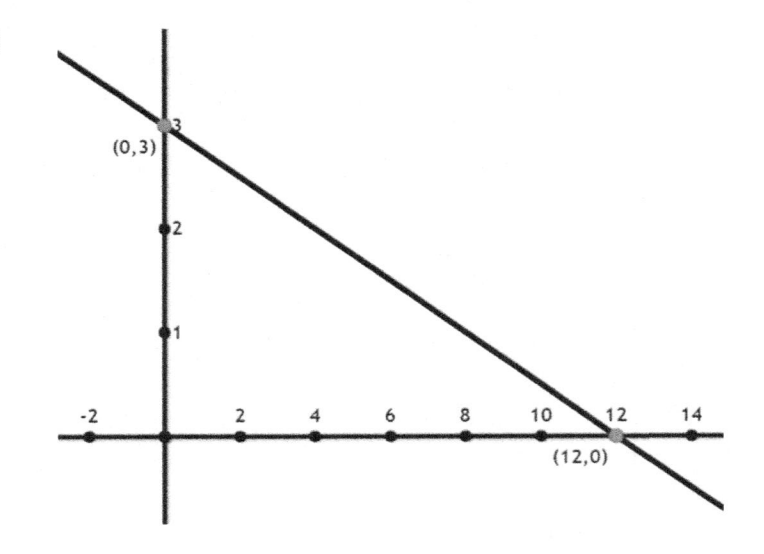

(0,3)

(12,0)

✎ Sketch the graph of each line.

1)

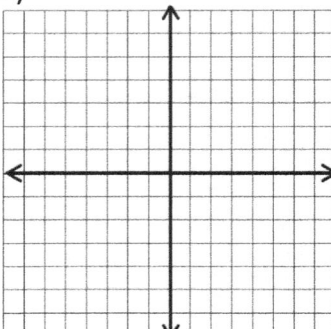

2)

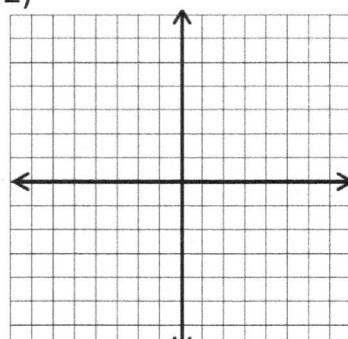

Writing Linear Equations

Helpful Hints

The equation of a line:
$$y = mx + b$$

1– Identify the slope.

2– Find the y–intercept. This can be done by substituting the slope and the coordinates of a point (x, y) on the line.

Example:

through:

$(-4, -2), (-3, 5)$

$y = 7x + 26$

✎ **Write the slope–intercept form of the equation of the line through the given points.**

1) through: $(-4, -2), (-3, 5)$

2) through: $(5, 4), (-4, 3)$

3) through: $(0, -2), (-5, 3)$

4) through: $(-1, 1), (-2, 6)$

5) through: $(0, 3), (-4, -1)$

6) through: $(0, 2), (1, -3)$

7) through: $(0, -5), (4, 3)$

8) through: $(-1, 4), (0, 4)$

9) through: $(2, -3), (3, -5)$

10) through: $(2, 5), (-1, -4)$

11) through: $(1, -3), (-3, 1)$

12) through: $(3, 3), (1, -5)$

13) through: $(4, 4), (3, -5)$

14) through: $(0, 3), (1, 1)$

15) through: $(5, 5), (2, -3)$

16) through: $(-2, -2), (2, -5)$

17) through: $(-3, -2), (1, -1)$

18) through: $(-2, 1), (6, 5)$

Graphing Linear Inequalities

Helpful Hints

1– First, graph the "equals" line.

2– Choose a testing point. (it can be any point on both sides of the line.)

3– Put the value of (x, y) of that point in the inequality. If that works, that part of the line is the solution. If the values don't work, then the other part of the line is the solution.

✎ Sketch the graph of each linear inequality.

1)

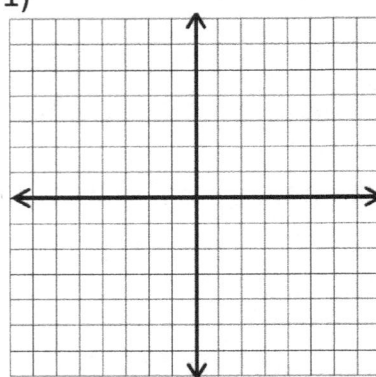

2)

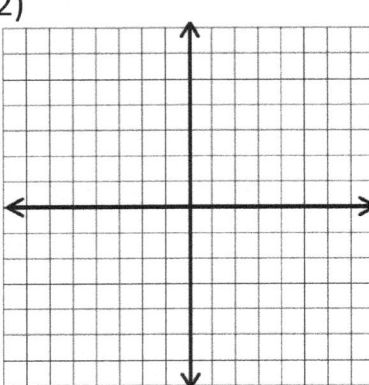

4)

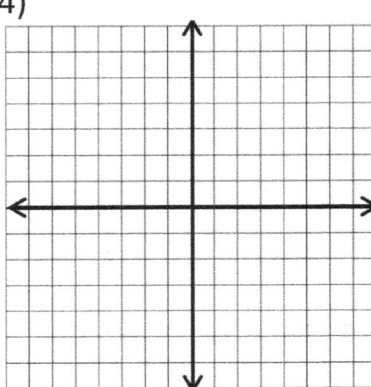

5)

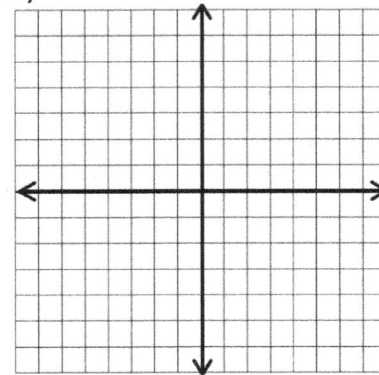

Finding Midpoint

> **Helpful Hints**
>
> Midpoint of the segment AB:
>
> $M\left(\dfrac{x_1+x_2}{2}, \dfrac{y_1+y_2}{2}\right)$
>
> Example:
>
> (3, 9), (− 1, 6)
>
> M (1, 7.5)

✎ **Find the midpoint of the line segment with the given endpoints.**

1) (2, − 2), (3, − 5)

2) (0, 2), (− 2, − 6)

3) (7, 4), (9, − 1)

4) (4, − 5), (0, 8)

5) (1, − 2), (1, − 6)

6) (− 2, − 3), (3, − 6)

7) (7, 0), (− 7, 5)

8) (− 2, 6), (− 3, − 2)

9) (− 1, 1), (5, − 5)

10) (2.3, − 1.3), (− 2.2, − 0.5)

11) (4.1, 6.32), (4, 5.6)

12) (2, − 1), (− 6, 0)

13) (− 4, 4), (5, − 1)

14) (− 2, − 3), (− 6, 5)

15) $\left(\dfrac{1}{2}, 1\right)$, (2, 4)

16) (− 2, − 2), (6, 5)

Finding Distance of Two Points

Helpful Hints

Distance from A to B:

$$d = \sqrt{(x_1 - x_2)^2 + (y_1 - y_2)^2}$$

Example:

$(-1, 2), (-1, -7)$

Distance = 9

✎ Find the distance between each pair of points.

1) $(2, -1), (1, -1)$

2) $(6, 4), (-1, 3)$

3) $(-8, -5), (-6, 1)$

4) $(-6, -10), (-2, -10)$

5) $(4, -6), (-3, 4)$

6) $(-6, -7), (-2, -8)$

7) $(5, 4), (8, 2)$

8) $(8, 4), (3, -7)$

9) $(1, 3), (5, 7)$

10) $(4, 2), (-7, 1)$

11) $(-3, -4), (-7, -2)$

12) $(-7, -2), (6, 9)$

13) $(10, 0), (0, 4)$

14) $(-3, 2), (5, 0)$

15) $(-5, 6), (8, -4)$

16) $(3, -5), (-8, -4)$

17) $(0, 8), (4, 10)$

18) $(6, 4), (-5, -1)$

Answers of Worksheets – Day 4

The Distributive Property

1) 5x + 2
2) 6x − 2
3) −5x + 10
4) 3x − 7
5) 16x + 64
6) 4x + 24
7) − 24x + 32
8) 42x − 21
9) − 24x − 12
10) − 18x + 72
11) − 38x² − 14x
12) − 27x + 15
13) − 5x − 10
14) − 6x + 14
15) − 16x + 13
16) − 6x − 14

Evaluating One Variable

1) 6
2) 7
3) 25
4) −7
5) 18
6) 2
7) 10
8) −14
9) 1
10) 33
11) 1
12) −8
13) −5
14) 0
15) −176

Evaluating Two Variables

1) 21
2) 39
3) 64
4) 26
5) 45
6) −111
7) 56
8) 6
9) 58
10) 17

Combining like Terms

1) 2x − 3
2) −4x + 12
3) 9x + 3
4) −15x − 28
5) 2x − 5
6) −11x
7) 23x + 42
8) −21x
9) −2x − 12
10) 4x + 8
11) −14x
12) − x + 8
13) 10x − 6
14) 42x − 5
15) 24x + 6
16) −27x
17) 9x − 9
18) x
19) 2x + 12
20) 12x − 9
21) x

One–Step Equations

1) 14
2) 30
3) − 10
4) 6
5) − 10
6) − 4
7) − 11
8) 13
9) 4
10) − 9
11) − 13
12) − 9
13) − 8
14) 4
15) − 6
16) 11
17) 50
18) 4
19) − 9
20) 17
21) 10

Two–Step Equations

1) − 4
2) 3
3) 2
4) 1
5) 0.5
6) $\frac{4}{3}$
7) $-\frac{73}{8}$
8) $\frac{2}{5}$
9) − 1
10) 12
11) − 87
12) − 8
13) 128
14) 32
15) − 48
16) 10
17) − 1
18) − 5
19) − 31
20) − 24

Multi–Step Equations

1) 6
2) 2
3) − 2
4) 2
5) − 20
6) 37
7) 22
8) $\frac{4}{3}$
9) − 4
10) − 8
11) − 6
12) 2
13) 8
14) 1
15) 5
16) − 6
17) − 8
18) − 1
19) − 1
20) 0

Graphing Single–Variable Inequalities

1) $-2 > x$

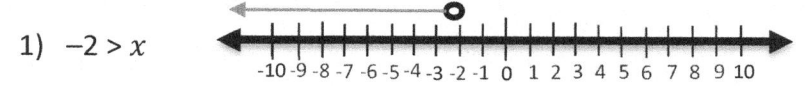

2) $x \leq -5$

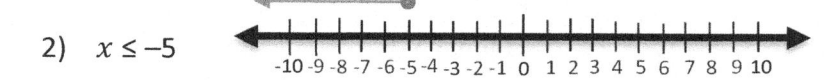

3) $x > 7$

4) $-1.5 > x$

One–Step Inequalities

1) $x + 9 \geq 11$

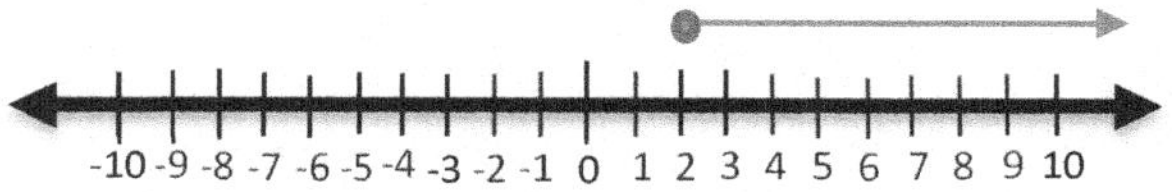

2) $x - 4 \leq 2$

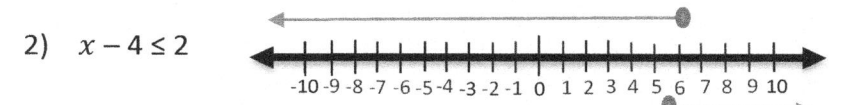

3) $6x \geq 36$

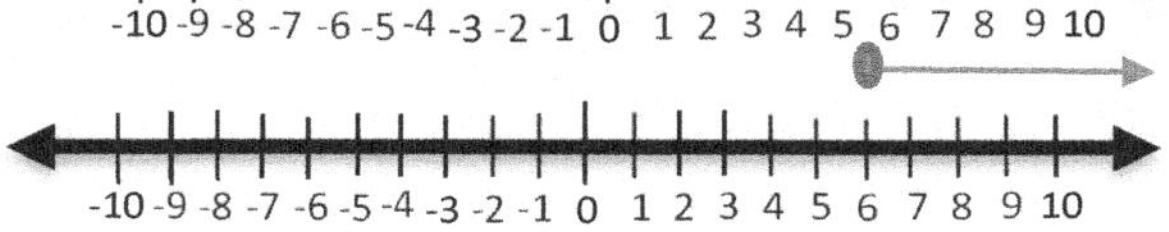

4) $7 + x < 16$

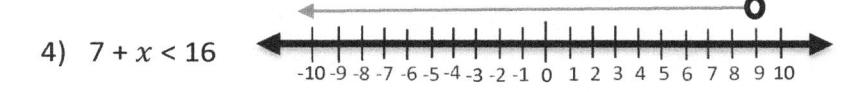

5) $x + 8 \leq 1$

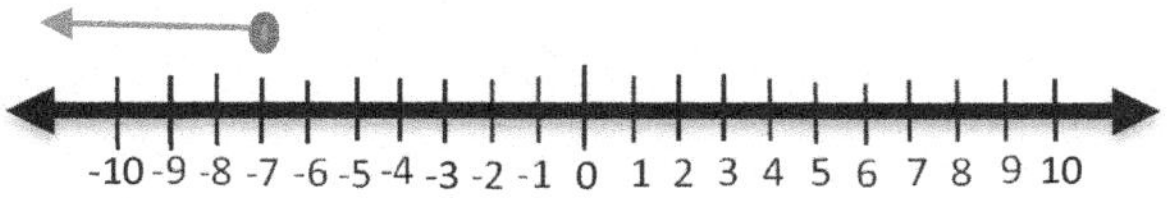

6) $3x > 12$

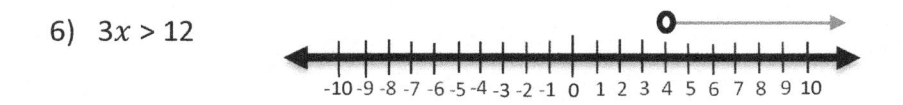

7) $3x < 24$

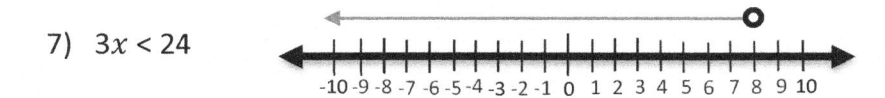

Two–Step inequalities

1) $x \leq 3$
2) $x \leq 4$
3) $x \leq 3$
4) $x \geq 2$
5) $x \geq 4$
6) $x \leq 5$
7) $x \leq 1$
8) $x \leq 1$
9) $x \leq 1$
10) $x \leq 1$
11) $x < 9.5$
12) $x < 12$
13) $x \geq 3$
14) $x < 3$
15) $x \geq 8$
16) $x < 4$

Multi–Step inequalities

1) $x < 7$
2) $x \leq 4$
3) $x > 5$
4) $x < 0$
5) $x < 9$
6) $x \leq 17$

Finding Slope

1) 2
2) $\frac{2}{7}$
3) -11
4) 0
5) $-\frac{1}{32}$
6) 1
7) $-\frac{3}{2}$
8) -1
9) $-\frac{1}{3}$
10) $\frac{11}{2}$
11) $-\frac{1}{17}$
12) $-\frac{22}{23}$
13) $-\frac{3}{4}$
14) $-\frac{5}{8}$
15) $-\frac{1}{14}$
16) $\frac{11}{20}$
17) Undefined
18) $-\frac{3}{19}$

Graphing Lines Using Slope–Intercept Form

1)

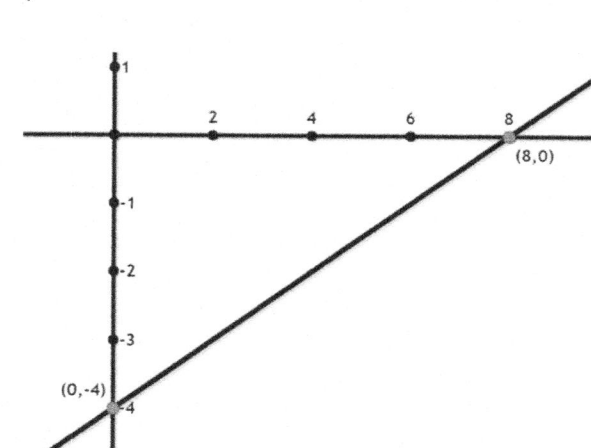

2)

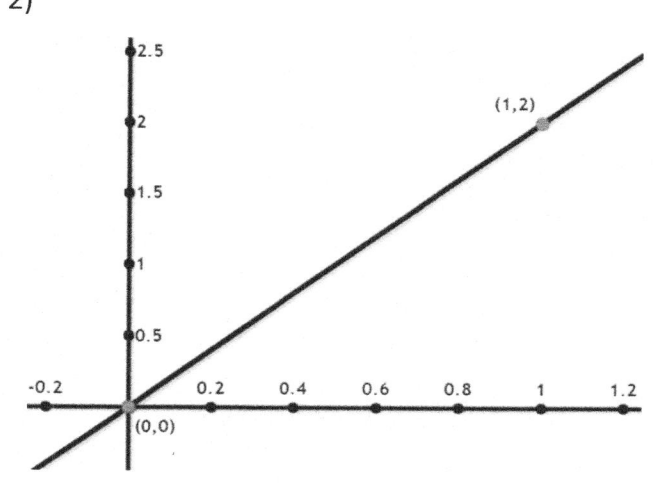

Graphing Lines Using Standard Form

1)

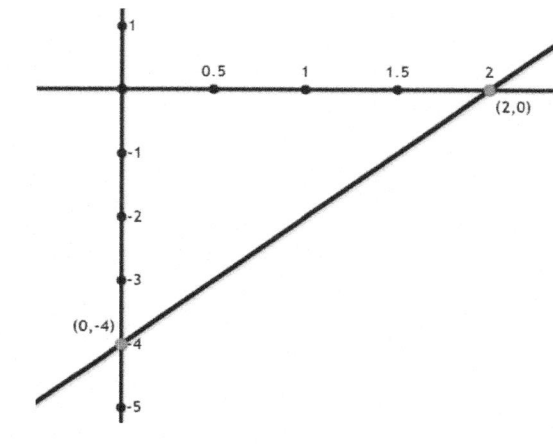

2)

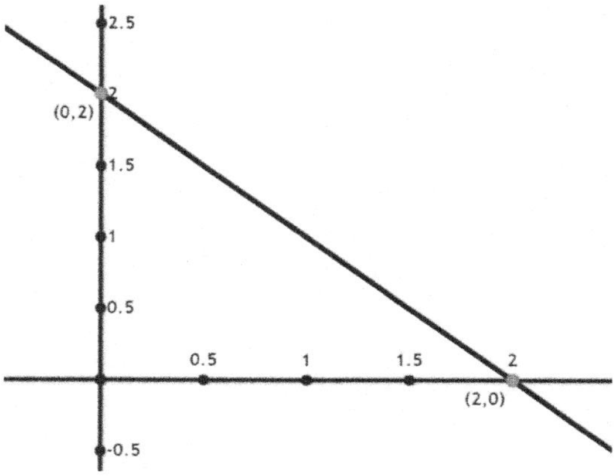

Writing Linear Equations

1) $y = 7x + 26$
2) $y = \frac{1}{9}x + \frac{31}{9}$
3) $y = -x - 2$
4) $y = -5x - 4$
5) $y = x + 3$
6) $y = -5x + 2$
7) $y = 2x - 5$
8) $y = 4$
9) $y = -2x + 1$
10) $y = 3x - 1$
11) $y = -x - 2$
12) $y = 4x - 9$
13) $y = 9x - 32$
14) $y = -2x + 3$
15) $y = \frac{8}{3}x - \frac{25}{3}$
16) $y = -\frac{3}{4}x - \frac{7}{2}$
17) $y = \frac{1}{4}x - \frac{5}{4}$
18) $y = -\frac{4}{3}x + \frac{19}{3}$

Graphing Linear Inequalities

1)

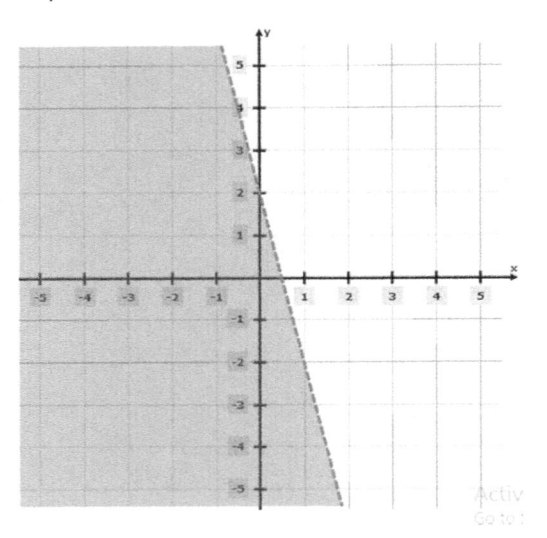

2)

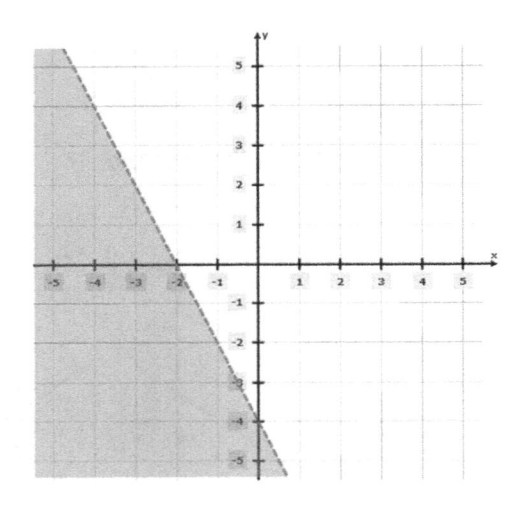

4)

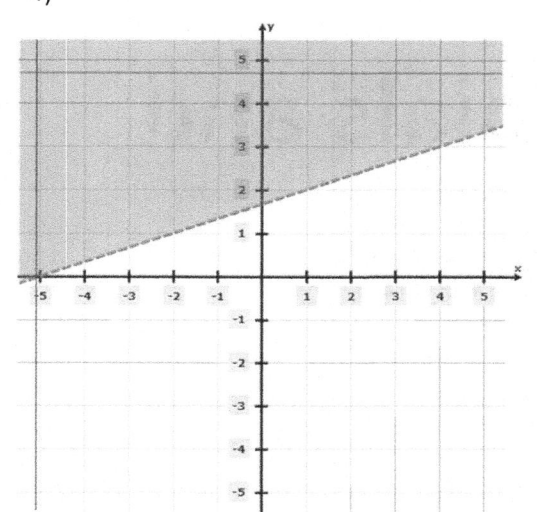

5)

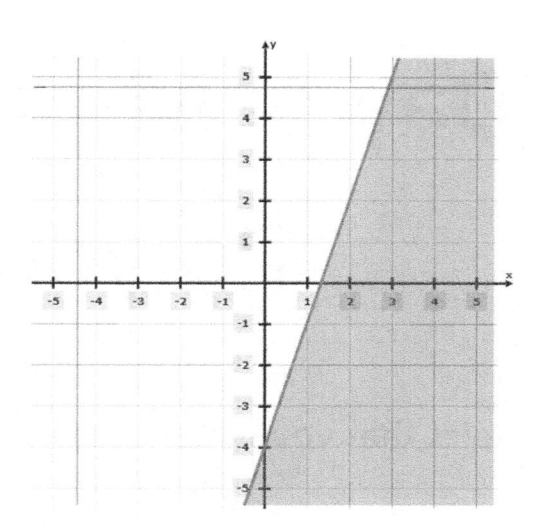

Finding Midpoint

1) (2.5, −3.5)
2) (−1, −2)
3) (8, 1.5)
4) (2, 1.5)
5) (1, −4)
6) (0.5, −4.5)
7) (0, 2.5)
8) (−2.5, 2)
9) (2, −2)
10) (0.05, −0.9)
11) (4.05, 5.96)
12) (−2, − 0.5)
13) $(\frac{1}{2}, 1\frac{1}{2})$
14) (−4, 1)
15) (1.25, 2.5)
16) $(2, \frac{3}{2})$

Finding Distance of Two Points

1) 1
2) 7.1
3) 6.32
4) 4
5) 12.21
6) 4.12
7) 3.61
8) 12.1
9) 5.66
10) 11.04
11) 4.47
12) 17.03
13) 10.77
14) 8.25
15) 16.4
16) 10.3
17) 4.47
18) 12.1

Day 4: Monomials and Polynomials

Math Topics that you'll learn today:

- Writing Linear Equations
- Graphing Linear Inequalities
- Finding Midpoint
- Finding Distance of Two Points
- Classifying Polynomials
- Writing Polynomials in Standard Form
- Simplifying Polynomials
- Adding and Subtracting Polynomials
- Multiplying Monomials
- Multiplying and Dividing Monomials
- Multiplying a Polynomial and a Monomial
- Multiplying Binomials
- Factoring Trinomials
- Operations with Polynomials
- Solve a Quadratic Equation
- Is (x, y) a solution to the system of equations?
- Solving Systems of Equations

Mathematics – the unshaken Foundation of Sciences, and the plentiful Fountain of Advantage to human affairs. — Isaac Barrow

Classifying Polynomials

Helpful Hints

Name	Degree	Example
constant	0	4
linear	1	$2x$
quadratic	2	$x^2 + 5x + 6$
cubic	3	$x^3 - x^2 + 4x + 8$
quartic	4	$x^4 + 3x^3 - x^2 + 2x + 6$
quantic	5	$x^5 - 2x^4 + x^3 - x^2 + x + 10$

✎Name each polynomial by degree and number of terms.

1) x

2) $-5x^4$

3) $7x - 4$

4) -6

5) $8x + 1$

6) $9x^2 - 8x^3$

7) $2x^5$

8) $10 + 8x$

9) $5x^2 - 6x$

10) $-7x^7 + 7x^4$

11) $-8x^4 + 5x^3 - 2x^2 - 8x$

12) $4x - 9x^2 + 4x^3 - 5x^4$

13) $4x^6 + 5x^5 + x^4$

14) $-4 - 2x^2 + 8x$

15) $9x^6 - 8$

16) $7x^5 + 10x^4 - 3x + 10x^7$

17) $4x^6 - 3x^2 - 8x^4$

18) $-5x^4 + 10x - 10$

Writing Polynomials in Standard Form

Helpful Hints

A polynomial function $f(x)$ of degree n is of the form

$f(x) = a_n x^n + a_{n-1} x^{n-1} + \ldots + a_1 x + a_0$

The first term is the one with the biggest power!

Example:

$2x^2 - 4x^3 - x =$

$-4x^3 + 2x^2 - x$

✎ *Write each polynomial in standard form.*

1) $3x^2 - 5x^3$

2) $3 + 4x^3 - 3$

3) $2x^2 + 1x - 6x^3$

4) $9x - 7x$

5) $12 - 7x + 9x^4$

6) $5x^2 + 13x - 2x^3$

7) $-3 + 16x - 16x$

8) $3x(x + 4) - 2(x + 4)$

9) $(x + 5)(x - 2)$

10) $3x^2 + x + 12 - 5x^2 - 2x$

11) $12x^5 + 7x^3 - 3x^5 - 8x^3$

12) $3x(2x + 5 - 2x^2)$

13) $11x(x^5 + 2x^3)$

14) $(x + 6)(x + 3)$

15) $(x + 4)^2$

16) $(8x - 7)(3x + 2)$

17) $5x(3x^2 + 2x + 1)$

18) $7x(3 - x + 6x^3)$

Simplifying Polynomials

Helpful Hints

1– Find "like" terms. (they have same variables with same power).

2– Add or Subtract "like" terms using PEMDAS operation.

Example:

$2x^5 - 3x^3 + 8x^2 - 2x^5 =$

$-3x^3 + 8x^2$

✎ *Simplify each expression.*

1) $11 - 4x^2 + 3x^2 - 7x^3 + 3$

2) $2x^5 - x^3 + 8x^2 - 2x^5$

3) $(-5)(x^6 + 10) - 8(14 - x^6)$

4) $4(2x^2 + 4x^2 - 3x^3) + 6x^3 + 17$

5) $11 - 6x^2 + 5x^2 - 12x^3 + 22$

6) $2x^2 - 2x + 3x^3 + 12x - 22x$

7) $(3x - 8)(3x - 4)$

8) $(12x + 2y)^2$

9) $(12x^3 + 28x^2 + 10x + 4) \div (x + 2)$

10) $(2x + 12x^2 - 2) \div (2x + 1)$

11) $(2x^3 - 1) + (3x^3 - 2x^3)$

12) $(x - 5)(x - 3)$

13) $(3x + 8)(3x - 8)$

14) $(8x^2 - 3x) - (5x - 5 - 8x^2)$

Adding and Subtracting Polynomials

Helpful Hints

Adding polynomials is just a matter of combining like terms, with some order of operations considerations thrown in.

Be careful with the minus signs, and don't confuse addition and multiplication!

Example:

$(3x^3 - 1) - (4x^3 + 2)$

$= -x^3 - 3$

✏️ *Simplify each expression.*

1) $(2x^3 - 2) + (2x^3 + 2)$

2) $(4x^3 + 5) - (7 - 2x^3)$

3) $(4x^2 + 2x^3) - (2x^3 + 5)$

4) $(4x^2 - x) + (3x - 5x^2)$

5) $(7x + 9) - (3x + 9)$

6) $(4x^4 - 2x) - (6x - 2x^4)$

7) $(12x - 4x^3) - (8x^3 + 6x)$

8) $(2x^3 - 8x^2) - (5x^2 - 3x^3)$

9) $(2x^2 - 6) + (9x^2 - 4x^3)$

10) $(4x^3 + 3x^4) - (x^4 - 5x^3)$

11) $(-12x^4 + 10x^5 + 2x^3) + (14x^3 + 23x^5 + 8x^4)$

12) $(13x^2 - 6x^5 - 2x) - (-10x^2 - 11x^5 + 9x)$

13) $(35 + 9x^5 - 3x^2) + (8x^4 + 3x^5) - (27 - 5x^4)$

14) $(3x^5 - 2x^3 - 4x) + (4x + 10x^4 - 23) + (x^2 - x^3 + 12)$

Multiplying Monomials

Helpful Hints

A monomial is a polynomial with just one term, like $2x$ or $7y$.

Example:

$2u^3 \times (-3u)$

$= -6u^4$

✎ Simplify each expression.

1) $2xy^2z \times 4z^2$

2) $4xy \times x^2y$

3) $4pq^3 \times (-2p^4q)$

4) $8s^4t^2 \times st^5$

5) $12p^3 \times (-3p^4)$

6) $-4p^2q^3r \times 6pq^2r^3$

7) $(-8a^4) \times (-12a^6b)$

8) $3u^4v^2 \times (-7u^2v^3)$

9) $4u^3 \times (-2u)$

10) $-6xy^2 \times 3x^2y$

11) $12y^2z^3 \times (-y^2z)$

12) $5a^2bc^2 \times 2abc^2$

Multiplying and Dividing Monomials

Helpful Hints
- When you divide two monomials you need to divide their coefficients and then divide their variables.
- In case of exponents with the same base, you need to subtract their powers.

Example:

$(-3x^2)(8x^4y^{12}) = -24x^6y^{12}$

$\dfrac{36\ x^5y^7}{4\ x^4y^5} = 9xy^2$

✍ Simplify.

1) $(7x^4y^6)(4x^3y^4)$

2) $(15x^4)(3x^9)$

3) $(12x^2y^9)(7x^9y^{12})$

4) $\dfrac{80\ x^{12}y^9}{10\ x^6y^7}$

5) $\dfrac{95\ x^{18}y^7}{5\ x^9y^2}$

6) $\dfrac{200\ x^3y^8}{40\ x^3y^7}$

7) $\dfrac{-15\ x^{17}y^{13}}{3\ x^6y^9}$

8) $\dfrac{-64\ x^8y^{10}}{8\ x^3y^7}$

Multiplying a Polynomial and a Monomial

Helpful Hints

– When multiplying monomials, use the product rule for exponents.

– When multiplying a monomial by a polynomial, use the distributive property.

a × (b + c) = a × b + a × c

Example:

$2x(8x - 2) =$

$16x^2 - 4x$

✎ Find each product.

1) $5(3x - 6y)$

2) $9x(2x + 4y)$

3) $8x(7x - 4)$

4) $12x(3x + 9)$

5) $11x(2x - 11y)$

6) $2x(6x - 6y)$

7) $3x(2x^2 - 3x + 8)$

8) $13x(4x + 8y)$

9) $20(2x^2 - 8x - 5)$

10) $3x(3x - 2)$

11) $6x^3(3x^2 - 2x + 2)$

12) $8x^2(3x^2 - 5xy + 7y^2)$

13) $2x^2(3x^2 - 5x + 12)$

14) $2x^3(2x^2 + 5x - 4)$

15) $5x(6x^2 - 5xy + 2y^2)$

16) $9(x^2 + xy - 8y^2)$

Multiplying Binomials

Helpful Hints

Use "FOIL". (First–Out–In–Last)

$(x + a)(x + b) = x^2 + (b + a)x + ab$

Example:

$(x + 2)(x - 3) =$

$x^2 - x - 6$

✍ Multiply.

1) $(3x - 2)(4x + 2)$

2) $(2x - 5)(x + 7)$

3) $(x + 2)(x + 8)$

4) $(x^2 + 2)(x^2 - 2)$

5) $(x - 2)(x + 4)$

6) $(x - 8)(2x + 8)$

7) $(5x - 4)(3x + 3)$

8) $(x - 7)(x - 6)$

9) $(6x + 9)(4x + 9)$

10) $(2x - 6)(5x + 6)$

11) $(x - 7)(x + 7)$

12) $(x + 4)(4x - 8)$

13) $(6x - 4)(6x + 4)$

14) $(x - 7)(x + 2)$

15) $(x - 8)(x + 8)$

16) $(3x + 3)(3x - 4)$

17) $(x + 3)(x + 3)$

18) $(x + 4)(x + 6)$

Factoring Trinomials

Helpful Hints

"FOIL"

$(x + a)(x + b) = x^2 + (b + a)x + ab$

"Difference of Squares"

$a^2 - b^2 = (a + b)(a - b)$

$a^2 + 2ab + b^2 = (a + b)(a + b)$

$a^2 - 2ab + b^2 = (a - b)(a - b)$

"Reverse FOIL"

$x^2 + (b + a)x + ab = (x + a)(x + b)$

Example:

$x^2 + 5x + 6 =$

$(x + 2)(x + 3)$

✎ Factor each trinomial.

1) $x^2 - 7x + 12$

2) $x^2 + 5x - 14$

3) $x^2 - 11x - 42$

4) $6x^2 + x - 12$

5) $x^2 - 17x + 30$

6) $x^2 + 8x + 15$

7) $3x^2 + 11x - 4$

8) $x^2 - 6x - 27$

9) $10x^2 + 33x - 7$

10) $x^2 + 24x + 144$

11) $49x^2 + 28xy + 4y^2$

12) $16x^2 - 40x + 25$

13) $x^2 - 10x + 25$

14) $25x^2 - 20x + 4$

15) $x^3 + 6x^2y^2 + 9xy^3$

16) $9x^2 + 24x + 16$

17) $x^2 - 8x + 16$

18) $x^2 + 121 + 22x$

Operations with Polynomials

Helpful Hints

– When multiplying a monomial by a polynomial, use the distributive property.

a × (b + c) = a × b + a × c

Example:

5 (6x − 1) =

30x − 5

✏ **Find each product.**

1) $3x^2 (6x - 5)$

2) $5x^2 (7x - 2)$

3) $- 3 (8x - 3)$

4) $6x^3 (- 3x + 4)$

5) $9 (6x + 2)$

6) $8 (3x + 7)$

7) $5 (6x - 1)$

8) $- 7x^4 (2x - 4)$

9) $8 (x^2 + 2x - 3)$

10) $4 (4x^2 - 2x + 1)$

11) $2 (3x^2 + 2x - 2)$

12) $8x (5x^2 + 3x + 8)$

13) $(9x + 1)(3x - 1)$

14) $(4x + 5)(6x - 5)$

15) $(7x + 3)(5x - 6)$

16) $(3x - 4)(3x + 8)$

Solve a Quadratic Equation

Helpful Hints

Write the equation in the form of $ax^2 + bx + c = 0$

Factorize the quadratic.

Use quadratic formula if you couldn't factorize the quadratic.

Quadratic formula

$$x = \frac{-b \pm \sqrt{b^2 - 4ac}}{2a}$$

Example:

$x^2 + 5x + 6 = 0$

$(x + 3)(x + 2) = 0$

$(x + 3) = 0$

$x = -3$

$x + 2 = 0$

$x = -2$

✎ Solve each equation.

1) $(x + 2)(x - 4) = 0$

2) $(x + 5)(x + 8) = 0$

3) $(3x + 2)(x + 3) = 0$

4) $(4x + 7)(2x + 5) = 0$

5) $x^2 - 11x + 19 = -5$

6) $x^2 + 7x + 18 = 8$

7) $x^2 - 10x + 22 = -2$

8) $x^2 + 3x - 12 = 6$

9) $18x^2 + 45x - 27 = 0$

10) $90x^2 - 84x = -18$

11) $x^2 + 8x = -15$

Is (x, y) a solution to the system of equations?

Helpful Hints

The elimination method for solving systems of linear equations uses the addition property of equality. You can add the same value to each side of an equation.

Example:

Is (1, 2) a solution to this system of equations

$$x + 2y = 5$$
$$-x + y = 1$$

1 + 2 (2) = 5

−(1) + 2 = 1

Yes!

1) Is (1, 2) a solution to this system of equations?

$$5x + 2y = 9$$
$$15x + 7y = 29$$

2) Is (2, −3) a solution to the system of equations?

$$7x + 5y = 1$$
$$x + y = 1$$

3) Is (4, 3) a solution to the system of equations?

$$2x - 3y = -1$$
$$y = x - 1$$

4) Is (2, 3) a solution to the system of equations?

$$y = 5x - 7$$
$$-3x - 2y = -6$$

5) Is (0, −3) a solution to the system of equations?

$$-5x + y = -3$$
$$3x - 8y = 24$$

Solving Systems of Equations

Helpful Hints

The elimination method for solving systems of linear equations uses the addition property of equality. You can add the same value to each side of an equation.

Example:
$$x + 2y = 6$$
$$+\ -x + y = 3$$
$$3y = 9$$
$$y = 3$$
$$x + 6 = 6$$
$$x = 0$$

✎ Solve each system of equation.

1) $10x - 9y = -12$
   $-5x + 3y = 6$

2) $-3x - 4y = 5$
   $x - 2y = 5$

3) $5x - 14y = 22$
   $-6x + 7y = 3$

4) $10x - 14y = -4$
   $-10x - 20y = -30$

5) $32x + 14y = 52$
   $16x - 4y = -40$

6) $2x - 8y = -6$
   $8x + 2y = 10$

7) $-4x + 4y = -4$
   $4x + 2y = 10$

8) $4x + 6y = 10$
   $8x + 12y = -20$

9) $20x - 18y = -12$
   $18x - 8y = 22$

10) $8x + 10y = 52$
    $8x + 6y = 44$

Answers of Worksheets – Day 5

Classifying Polynomials

1) Linear monomial
2) Quartic monomial
3) Linear binomial
4) Constant monomial
5) Linear binomial
6) Cubic binomial
7) Quantic monomial
8) Linear binomial
9) Quadratic binomial
10) Seventh degree binomial
11) Quartic polynomial with four terms
12) Quartic polynomial with four terms
13) Sixth degree trinomial
14) Quadratic trinomial
15) Sixth degree binomial
16) Seventh degree polynomial with four terms
17) Sixth degree trinomial
18) Quartic trinomial

Writing Polynomials in Standard Form

1) $-5x^3 + 3x^2$
2) $4x^3$
3) $-6x^3 + 2x^2 + x$
4) $2x$
5) $9x^4 - 7x + 12$
6) $-2x^3 + 5x^2 + 13x$
7) -3
8) $3x^2 + 10x - 8$
9) $x^2 + 3x - 10$
10) $-2x^2 - x + 12$
11) $9x^5 - x^3$
12) $-6x^3 + 6x^2 + 15x$
13) $11x^6 + 22x^4$
14) $x^2 + 9x + 18$
15) $x^2 + 8x + 16$
16) $24x^2 - 5x - 14$
17) $15x^3 + 10x^2 + 5x$
18) $42x^4 - 7x^2 + 21x$

Simplifying Polynomials

1) $-7x^3 - x^2 + 14$
2) $-x^3 + 8x^2$
3) $3x^6 - 162$
4) $-6x^3 + 24x^2 + 17$
5) $-12x^3 - x^2 + 33$
6) $3x^3 + 2x^2 - 12x$

7) $9x^2 - 36x + 32$

8) $144x^2 + 48xy + 4y^2$

9) $12x^2 + 4x + 2$

10) $6x - 1$

11) $3x^3 - 1$

12) $x^2 - 8x + 15$

13) $9x^2 - 64$

14) $16x^2 - 8x + 5$

Adding and Subtracting Polynomials

1) $4x^3$

2) $6x^3 - 2$

3) $4x^2 - 5$

4) $-x^2 + 2x$

5) $4x$

6) $6x^4 - 8x$

7) $-12x^3 + 6x$

8) $5x^3 - 13x^2$

9) $-4x^3 + 11x^2 - 6$

10) $2x^4 + 9x^3$

11) $33x^5 - 4x^4 + 16x^3$

12) $5x^5 + 23x^2 - 11x$

13) $12x^5 + 13x^4 - 3x^2 + 8$

14) $3x^5 + 10x^4 - 3x^3 + x^2 - 11$

Multiplying Monomials

1) $8xy^2z^3$

2) $4x^3y^2$

3) $-8p^5q^4$

4) $8s^5t^7$

5) $-36p^7$

6) $-24p^3q^5r^4$

7) $96a^{10}b$

8) $-21u^6v^5$

9) $-8u^4$

10) $-18x^3y^3$

11) $-12y^4z^4$

12) $10a^3b^2c^4$

Multiplying and Dividing Monomials

1) $28x^7y^{10}$

2) $45x^{13}$

3) $84x^{11}y^{21}$

4) $8x^6y^2$

5) $19x^9y^5$

6) $5y$

7) $-5x^{11}y^4$

8) $-8x^5y^3$

Multiplying a Polynomial and a Monomial

1) $15x - 30y$

2) $18x^2 + 36xy$

3) $56x^2 - 32x$

4) $36x^2 + 108x$

5) $22x^2 - 121xy$

6) $12x^2 - 12xy$

7) $6x^3 - 9x^2 + 24x$

8) $52x^2 + 104xy$

9) $40x^2 - 160x - 100$

10) $9x^2 - 6x$

11) $18x^5 - 12x^4 + 12x^3$
12) $24x^4 - 40x^3y + 56y^2x^2$
13) $6x^4 - 10x^3 + 24x^2$

14) $4x^5 + 10x^4 - 8x^3$
15) $30x^3 - 25x^2y + 10xy^2$
16) $9x^2 + 9xy - 72y^2$

Multiplying Binomials

1) $12x^2 - 2x - 4$
2) $2x^2 + 9x - 35$
3) $x^2 + 10x + 16$
4) $x^4 - 4$
5) $x^2 + 2x - 8$
6) $2x^2 - 8x - 64$
7) $15x^2 + 3x - 12$
8) $x^2 - 13x + 42$
9) $24x^2 + 90x + 81$

10) $10x^2 - 18x - 36$
11) $x^2 - 49$
12) $4x^2 + 8x - 32$
13) $36x^2 - 16$
14) $x^2 - 5x - 14$
15) $x^2 - 64$
16) $9x^2 - 3x - 12$
17) $x^2 + 6x + 9$
18) $x^2 + 10x + 24$

Factoring Trinomials

1) $(x - 3)(x - 4)$
2) $(x - 2)(x + 7)$
3) $(x + 3)(x - 14)$
4) $(2x + 3)(3x - 4)$
5) $(x - 15)(x - 2)$
6) $(x + 3)(x + 5)$
7) $(3x - 1)(x + 4)$
8) $(x - 9)(x + 3)$
9) $(5x - 1)(2x + 7)$

10) $(x + 12)(x + 12)$
11) $(7x + 2y)(7x + 2y)$
12) $(4x - 5)(4x - 5)$
13) $(x - 5)(x - 5)$
14) $(5x - 2)(5x - 2)$
15) $x(x^2 + 6xy^2 + 9y^3)$
16) $(3x + 4)(3x + 4)$
17) $(x - 4)(x - 4)$
18) $(x + 11)(x + 11)$

Operations with Polynomials

1) $18x^3 - 15x^2$
2) $35x^3 - 10x^2$
3) $-24x + 9$
4) $-18x^4 + 24x^3$
5) $54x + 18$
6) $24x + 56$

7) $30x - 5$
8) $-14x^5 + 28x^4$
9) $8x^2 + 16x - 24$
10) $16x^2 - 8x + 4$
11) $6x^2 + 4x - 4$
12) $40x^3 + 24x^2 + 64x$

13) $27x^2 - 6x - 1$

14) $24x^2 + 10x - 25$

15) $35x^2 - 27x - 18$

16) $9x^2 + 12x - 32$

Solving Quadratic Equations

1) $x = -2, x = 4$

2) $x = -5, x = -8$

3) $x = -\frac{2}{3}, x = -3$

4) $x = -\frac{7}{4}, x = -\frac{5}{2}$

5) $x = 8, x = 3$

6) $x = -5, x = -2$

7) $x = 6, x = 4$

8) $x = -6, x = 3$

9) $x = \frac{1}{2}, x = -3$

10) $x = \frac{3}{5}, x = \frac{1}{3}$

11) $x = -5, x = -3$

Is (x, y) a solution to the system of equations?

1) Yes
2) No

3) Yes
4) No

5) Yes

Solve each system of equations

1) $(-\frac{6}{5}, 0)$

2) $(1, -2)$

3) $(-4, -3)$

4) $(1, 1)$

5) $(-1, 6)$

6) $(1, 1)$

7) $(2, 1)$

8) No solution

9) $(3, 4)$

10) $(4, 2)$

Day 5: Exponents, Roots and Statistics

Math Topics that you'll learn today:

- ✓ Multiplication Property of Exponents
- ✓ Division Property of Exponents
- ✓ Powers of Products and Quotients
- ✓ Zero and Negative Exponents
- ✓ Negative Exponents and Negative Bases
- ✓ Writing Scientific Notation
- ✓ Square Roots
- ✓ Mean, Median, Mode, and Range of the Given Data
- ✓ Bar Graph
- ✓ Box and Whisker Plots
- ✓ Stem– And– Leaf Plot
- ✓ The Pie Graph or Circle Graph
- ✓ Scatter Plots
- ✓ Probability

Mathematics is no more computation than typing is literature.

– John Allen Paulos

Multiplication Property of Exponents

Helpful Hints

Exponents rules

$x^a \cdot x^b = x^{a+b}$ $x^a/x^b = x^{a-b}$

$1/x^b = x^{-b}$ $(x^a)^b = x^{a \cdot b}$

$(xy)^a = x^a \cdot y^a$

Example:

$(x^2y)^3 = x^6y^3$

✎ Simplify.

1) $4^2 \cdot 4^2$

2) $2 \cdot 2^2 \cdot 2^2$

3) $3^2 \cdot 3^2$

4) $3x^3 \cdot x$

5) $12x^4 \cdot 3x$

6) $6x \cdot 2x^2$

7) $5x^4 \cdot 5x^4$

8) $6x^2 \cdot 6x^3y^4$

9) $7x^2y^5 \cdot 9xy^3$

10) $7xy^4 \cdot 4x^3y^3$

11) $(2x^2)^2$

12) $3x^5y^3 \cdot 8x^2y^3$

13) $7x^3 \cdot 10y^3x^5 \cdot 8yx^3$

14) $(x^4)^3$

15) $(2x^2)^4$

16) $(x^2)^3$

17) $(6x)^2$

18) $3x^4y^5 \cdot 7x^2y^3$

Division Property of Exponents

Helpful Hints

$$\frac{x^a}{x^b} = x^{a-b}, x \neq 0$$

Example:

$$\frac{x^{12}}{x^5} = x^7$$

✎ Simplify.

1) $\frac{5^5}{5}$

2) $\frac{3}{3^5}$

3) $\frac{2^2}{2^3}$

4) $\frac{2^4}{2^2}$

5) $\frac{x}{x^3}$

6) $\frac{3x^3}{9x^4}$

7) $\frac{2x^{-5}}{9x^{-2}}$

8) $\frac{21x^8}{7x^3}$

9) $\frac{7x^6}{4x^7}$

10) $\frac{6x^2}{4x^3}$

11) $\frac{5x}{10^3}$

12) $\frac{3x^3}{2x^5}$

13) $\frac{12^3}{14x^6}$

14) $\frac{12x^3}{9y^8}$

15) $\frac{25xy^4}{5x^6y^2}$

16) $\frac{2x^4}{7x}$

17) $\frac{16^2 y^8}{4x^3}$

18) $\frac{12^4}{15^7 y^9}$

19) $\frac{12yx^4}{10yx^8}$

20) $\frac{16^4 y}{9x^8 y^2}$

21) $\frac{5x^8}{20x^8}$

106

Powers of Products and Quotients

Helpful Hints

For any nonzero numbers a and b and any integer x, $(ab)^x = a^x \cdot b^x$.

Example:

$(2x^2 \cdot y^3)^2 =$

$4x^2 \cdot y^6$

✎ Simplify.

1) $(2x^3)^4$

2) $(4xy^4)^2$

3) $(5x^4)^2$

4) $(11x^5)^2$

5) $(4x^2y^4)^4$

6) $(2x^4y^4)^3$

7) $(3x^2y^2)^2$

8) $(3x^4y^3)^4$

9) $(2x^6y^8)^2$

10) $(12x\ 3x)^3$

11) $(2x^9\ x^6)^3$

12) $(5x^{10}y^3)^3$

13) $(4x^3\ x^2)^2$

14) $(3x^3\ 5x)^2$

15) $(10x^{11}y^3)^2$

16) $(9x^7\ y^{\ 5})^2$

17) $(4x^4y^6)^5$

18) $(4x^4)^2$

19) $(3x\ 4y^3)^2$

20) $(9x^2y)^3$

21) $(12x^2y^5)^2$

107

ACCUPLACER Math in 7 Days

Zero and Negative Exponents

Helpful Hints

A negative exponent simply means that the base is on the wrong side of the fraction line, so you need to flip the base to the other side. For instance, "x^{-2}" (pronounced as "ecks to the minus two") just means "x^2" but underneath, as in $\frac{1}{x^2}$

Example:

$5^{-2} = \frac{1}{25}$

✎ Evaluate the following expressions.

1) 8^{-2}

2) 2^{-4}

3) 10^{-2}

4) 5^{-3}

5) 22^{-1}

6) 9^{-1}

7) 3^{-2}

8) 4^{-2}

9) 5^{-2}

10) 35^{-1}

11) 6^{-3}

12) 0^{15}

13) 10^{-9}

14) 3^{-4}

15) 5^{-2}

16) 2^{-3}

17) 3^{-3}

18) 8^{-1}

19) 7^{-3}

20) 6^{-2}

21) $\left(\frac{2}{3}\right)^{-2}$

22) $\left(\frac{1}{5}\right)^{-3}$

23) $\left(\frac{1}{2}\right)^{-8}$

24) $\left(\frac{2}{5}\right)^{-3}$

www.EffortlessMath.com

Negative Exponents and Negative Bases

Helpful Hints

– Make the power positive. A negative exponent is the reciprocal of that number with a positive exponent.

– The parenthesis is important!

-5^{-2} is not the same as $(-5)^{-2}$

$-5^{-2} = -\frac{1}{5^2}$ and $(-5)^{-2} = +\frac{1}{5^2}$

Example:

$2x^{-3} = \frac{2}{x^3}$

✏ *Simplify.*

1) -6^{-1}

2) $-4x^{-3}$

3) $-\frac{5x}{x^{-3}}$

4) $-\frac{a^{-3}}{b^{-2}}$

5) $-\frac{5}{x^{-3}}$

6) $\frac{7b}{-9c^{-4}}$

7) $-\frac{5n^{-2}}{10p^{-3}}$

8) $\frac{4a^{-2}}{-3c^{-2}}$

9) $-12x^2y^{-3}$

10) $\left(-\frac{1}{3}\right)^{-2}$

11) $\left(-\frac{3}{4}\right)^{-2}$

12) $\left(\frac{3a}{2c}\right)^{-2}$

13) $\left(-\frac{5x}{3yz}\right)^{-3}$

14) $-\frac{2x}{a^{-4}}$

www.EffortlessMath.com

Writing Scientific Notation

Helpful Hints

– It is used to write very big or very small numbers in decimal form.

– In scientific notation all numbers are written in the form of:

$$m \times 10^n$$

Decimal notation	Scientific notation
5	5×10^0
−25,000	-2.5×10^4
0.5	5×10^{-1}
2,122.456	$2,122456 \times 10^3$

✎ *Write each number in scientific notation.*

1) 91×10^3

2) 60

3) 2000000

4) 0.0000006

5) 354000

6) 0.000325

7) 2.5

8) 0.00023

9) 56000000

10) 2000000

11) 78000000

12) 0.0000022

13) 0.00012

14) 0.004

15) 78

16) 1600

17) 1450

18) 130000

19) 60

20) 0.113

21) 0.02

Square Roots

Helpful Hints

– A square root of x is a number r whose square is: $r^2 = x$

r is a square root of x.

Example:

$\sqrt{4} = 2$

✏ Find the value each square root.

1) $\sqrt{1}$

2) $\sqrt{4}$

3) $\sqrt{9}$

4) $\sqrt{25}$

5) $\sqrt{16}$

6) $\sqrt{49}$

7) $\sqrt{36}$

8) $\sqrt{0}$

9) $\sqrt{64}$

10) $\sqrt{81}$

11) $\sqrt{121}$

12) $\sqrt{225}$

13) $\sqrt{144}$

14) $\sqrt{100}$

15) $\sqrt{256}$

16) $\sqrt{289}$

17) $\sqrt{324}$

18) $\sqrt{400}$

19) $\sqrt{900}$

20) $\sqrt{529}$

21) $\sqrt{90}$

Mean, Median, Mode, and Range of the Given Data

Helpful Hints

- Mean: $\frac{\text{sum of the data}}{\text{of data entires}}$
- Mode: value in the list that appears most often
- Range: largest value – smallest value

Example:

22, 16, 12, 9, 7, 6, 4, 6

Mean = 10.25

Mod = 6

Range = 18

✎ Find Mean, Median, Mode, and Range of the Given Data.

1) 7, 2, 5, 1, 1, 2

2) 2, 2, 2, 3, 6, 3, 7, 4

3) 9, 4, 3, 1, 7, 9, 4, 6, 4

4) 8, 4, 2, 4, 3, 2, 4, 5

5) 8, 5, 7, 5, 7, 9, 8

6) 5, 1, 4, 4, 9, 2, 9, 2, 5, 1

7) 4, 1, 5, 9, 7, 7, 5, 4, 3, 5

8) 7, 5, 4, 9, 6, 7, 7, 5, 2

9) 2, 5, 5, 6, 2, 4, 7, 6, 4, 9

10) 10, 5, 2, 5, 4, 5, 8, 10

11) 5, 1, 5, 2, 2

12) 2, 3, 5, 9, 6

Box and Whisker Plots

Helpful Hints

Box–and–whisker plots display data including quartiles.

- IQR – interquartile range shows the difference from Q1 to Q3.
- Extreme Values are the smallest and largest values in a data set.

Example:

73, 84, 86, 95, 68, 67, 100, 94, 77, 80, 62, 79

Maximum: 100, Minimum: 62, Q_1: 70.5, Q_2: 79.5, Q_3: 90

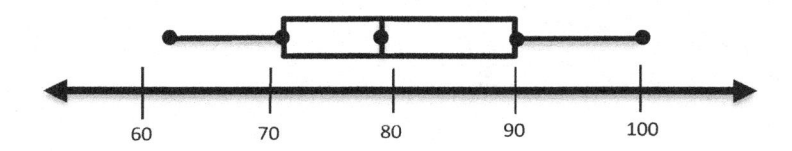

✎ *Make box and whisker plots for the given data.*

11, 17, 22, 18, 23, 2, 3, 16, 21, 7, 8, 15, 5

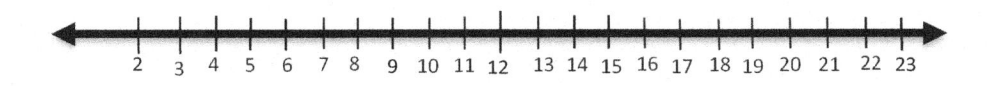

Bar Graph

Helpful Hints — A bar graph is a chart that presents data with bars in different heights to match with the values of the data. The bars can be graphed horizontally or vertically.

✎ Graph the given information as a bar graph.

Day	Hot dogs sold
Monday	90
Tuesday	70
Wednesday	30
Thursday	20
Friday	60

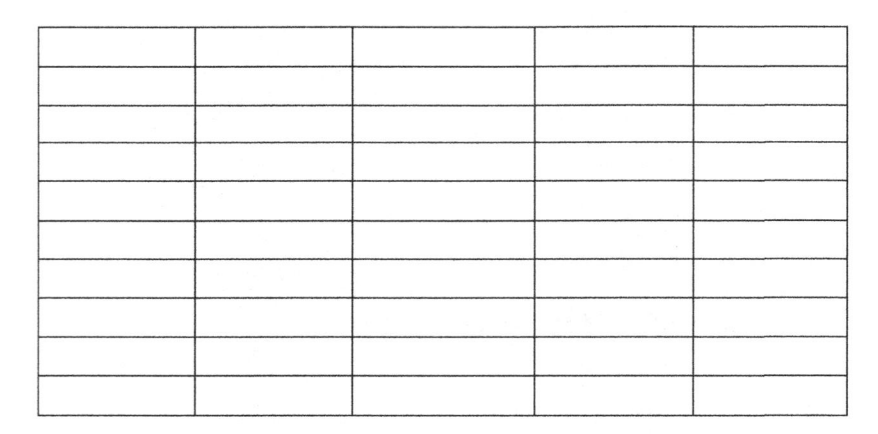

Monday   Tuesday   Wednesday   Thursday   Friday

Stem–And–Leaf Plot

Helpful Hints

– Stem–and–leaf plots display the frequency of the values in a data set.

– We can make a frequency distribution table for the values, or we can use a stem–and–leaf plot.

Example:

56, 58, 42, 48, 66, 64, 53, 69, 45, 72

Stem	leaf
4	2 5 8
5	3 6 8
6	4 6 9
7	2

✍ *Make stem ad leaf plots for the given data.*

1) 74, 88, 97, 72, 79, 86, 95, 79, 83, 91

Stem | Leaf plot

2) 37, 48, 26, 33, 49, 26, 19, 26, 48

Stem | Leaf plot

3) 58, 41, 42, 67, 54, 65, 65, 54, 69, 53

Stem | Leaf plot

The Pie Graph or Circle Graph

Helpful Hints

A Pie Chart is a circle chart divided into sectors, each sector represents the relative size of each value.

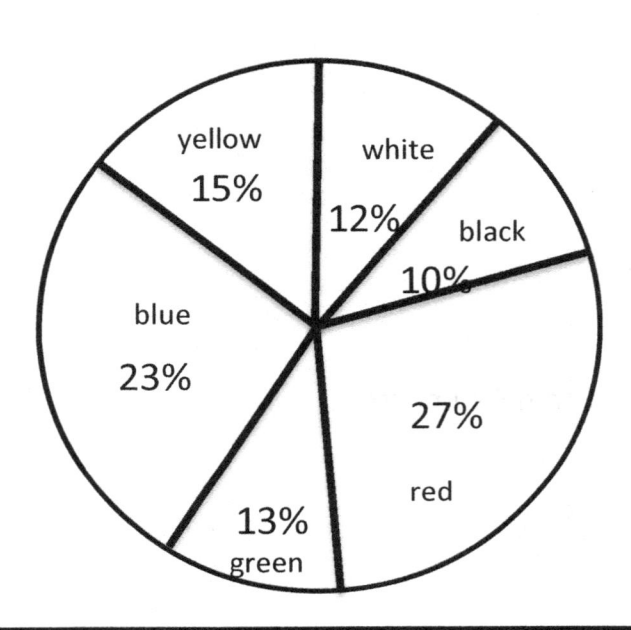

Pie chart:
- yellow 15%
- white 12%
- black 10%
- red 27%
- green 13%
- blue 23%

Favorite colors

1) Which color is the most?

2) What percentage of pie graph is yellow?

3) Which color is the least?

4) What percentage of pie graph is blue?

5) What percentage of pie graph is green?

116 www.EffortlessMath.com

Scatter Plots

> **Helpful Hints**
>
> A Scatter (xy) Plot shows the values with points that represent the relationship between two sets of data.
>
> — The horizontal values are usually x and vertical data is y.

✎ Construct a scatter plot.

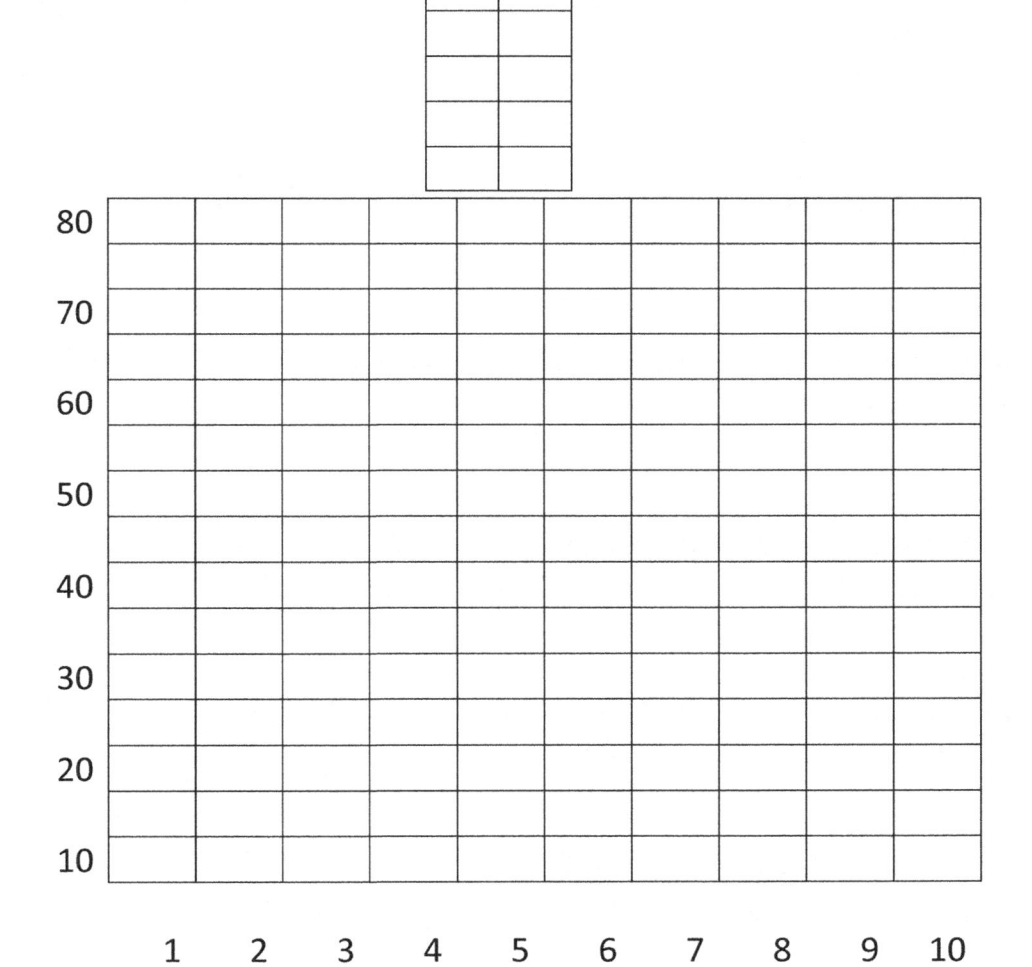

Probability Problems

> **Helpful Hints**
> - Probability is the likelihood of something happening in the future. It is expressed as a number between zero (can never happen) to 1 (will always happen).
> - Probability can be expressed as a fraction, a decimal, or a percent.
>
> **Example:**
>
> Probability of a flipped coins turns up 'heads'
>
> Is $0.5 = \frac{1}{2}$

✎ **Solve.**

1) A number is chosen at random from 1 to 10. Find the probability of selecting a 4 or smaller.

2) A number is chosen at random from 1 to 50. Find the probability of selecting multiples of 10.

3) A number is chosen at random from 1 to 10. Find the probability of selecting of 4 and factors of 6.

4) A number is chosen at random from 1 to 10. Find the probability of selecting a multiple of 3.

5) A number is chosen at random from 1 to 50. Find the probability of selecting prime numbers.

6) A number is chosen at random from 1 to 25. Find the probability of not selecting a composite number.

Answers of Worksheets – Day 6

Multiplication Property of Exponents

1) 4^4
2) 2^5
3) 3^4
4) $3x^4$
5) $36x^5$
6) $12x^3$
7) $25x^8$
8) $36x^5y^4$
9) $63x^3y^8$
10) $28x^4y^7$
11) $4x^4$
12) $24x^7y^6$
13) $560x^{11}y^4$
14) x^{12}
15) $16x^8$
16) x^6
17) $36x^2$
18) $21x^6y^8$

Division Property of Exponents

1) 5^4
2) $\frac{1}{3^4}$
3) $\frac{1}{2}$
4) 2^2
5) $\frac{1}{x^2}$
6) $\frac{1}{3x}$
7) $\frac{2}{9x^3}$
8) $3x^5$
9) $\frac{7}{4x}$
10) $\frac{3}{2x}$
11) $\frac{1}{2x^2}$
12) $\frac{3}{2x^2}$
13) $\frac{6}{7x^3}$
14) $\frac{4x^3}{3y^8}$
15) $\frac{5y^2}{x^5}$
16) $\frac{2x^3}{7}$
17) $\frac{4y^8}{x}$
18) $\frac{4}{5x^3y^9}$
19) $\frac{6}{5x^4}$
20) $\frac{16}{9x^4y}$
21) $\frac{1}{4}$

Powers of Products and Quotients

1) $16x^{12}$
2) $16x^2y^8$
3) $25x^8$
4) $121x^{10}$
5) $256x^8y^{16}$
6) $8x^{12}y^{12}$
7) $9x^4y^4$
8) $81x^{16}y^{12}$
9) $4x^{12}y^{16}$
10) $46,656x^6$
11) $8x^{45}$
12) $125x^{30}y^9$
13) $16x^{10}$
14) $225x^8$
15) $100x^{22}y^6$
16) $81x^{14}y^{10}$
17) $1,024x^{20}y^{30}$
18) $16x^8$
19) $144x^2y^6$
20) $729x^6y^3$
21) $144x^4y^{10}$

Zero and Negative Exponents

1) $\frac{1}{64}$
2) $\frac{1}{16}$
3) $\frac{1}{100}$
4) $\frac{1}{125}$
5) $\frac{1}{22}$
6) $\frac{1}{9}$
7) $\frac{1}{9}$
8) $\frac{1}{16}$
9) $\frac{1}{25}$
10) $\frac{1}{35}$
11) $\frac{1}{216}$
12) 0
13) $\frac{1}{1000000000}$
14) $\frac{1}{81}$
15) $\frac{1}{25}$
16) $\frac{1}{8}$
17) $\frac{1}{27}$
18) $\frac{1}{8}$
19) $\frac{1}{343}$
20) $\frac{1}{36}$
21) $\frac{9}{4}$
22) 125
23) 256
24) $\frac{125}{8}$

Negative Exponents and Negative Bases

1) $-\frac{1}{6}$
2) $-\frac{4}{x^3}$
3) $-5x^4$
4) $-\frac{b^2}{a^3}$
5) $-5x^3$
6) $-\frac{7bc^4}{9}$
7) $-\frac{p^3}{2n^2}$
8) $-\frac{4ac^2}{3b^2}$
9) $-\frac{12^2}{y^3}$
10) 9
11) $\frac{16}{9}$
12) $\frac{4c^2}{9a^2}$
13) $-\frac{27y^3z^3}{125x^3}$
14) $-2xa^4$

Writing Scientific Notation

1) 9.1×10^4
2) 6×10^1
3) 2×10^6
4) 6×10^{-7}
5) 3.54×10^5
6) 3.25×10^{-4}
7) 2.5×10^0
8) 2.3×10^{-4}
9) 5.6×10^7
10) 2×10^6
11) 7.8×10^7
12) 2.2×10^{-6}
13) 1.2×10^{-4}
14) 4×10^{-3}
15) 7.8×10^1
16) 1.6×10^3
17) 1.45×10^3
18) 1.3×10^5
19) 6×10^1
20) 1.13×10^{-1}
21) 2×10^{-2}

Square Roots

1) 1
2) 2
3) 3
4) 5
5) 4
6) 7
7) 6
8) 0
9) 8
10) 9
11) 11
12) 15
13) 12
14) 10
15) 16
16) 17
17) 18
18) 20
19) 30
20) 23
21) $3\sqrt{10}$

Mean, Median, Mode, and Range of the Given Data

1) mean: 3, median: 2, mode: 1, 2, range: 6
2) mean: 3.625, median: 3, mode: 2, range: 5
3) mean: 5.22, median: 4, mode: 4, range: 8
4) mean: 4, median: 4, mode: 4, range: 6
5) mean: 7, median: 7, mode: 5, 7, 8, range: 4
6) mean: 4.2, median: 4, mode: 1,2,4,5,9, range: 8
7) mean: 5, median: 5, mode: 5, range: 8
8) mean: 5.78, median: 6, mode: 7, range: 7
9) mean: 5, median: 5, mode: 2, 4, 5, 6, range: 7
10) mean: 6.125, median: 5, mode: 5, range: 8
11) mean: 3, median: 2, mode: 2, 5, range: 4
12) mean: 5, median: 5, mode: none, range: 7

Box and Whisker Plots

11, 17, 22, 18, 23, 2, 3, 16, 21, 7, 8, 15, 5

Maximum: 23, Minimum: 2, Q_1: 2, Q_2: 12.5, Q_3: 19.5

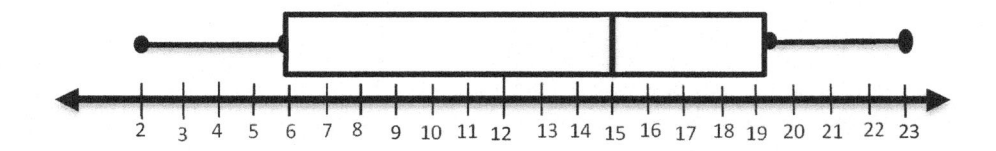

Bar Graph

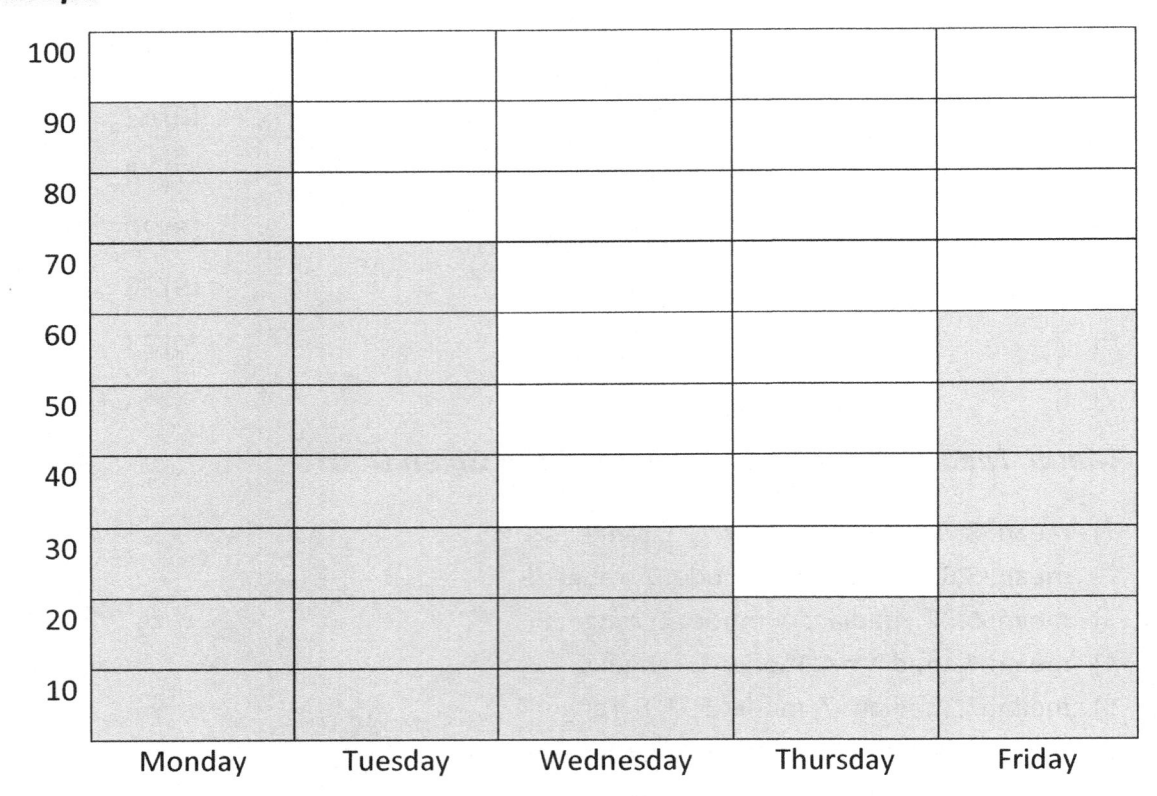

	Monday	Tuesday	Wednesday	Thursday	Friday
100					
90	■				
80	■				
70	■	■			
60	■	■			■
50	■	■			■
40	■	■			■
30	■	■	■		■
20	■	■	■	■	■
10	■	■	■	■	■

Stem–And–Leaf Plot

1)

Stem	leaf
7	2 4 9 9
8	3 6 8
9	1 5 7

2)

Stem	leaf
1	9
2	6 6 6
3	3 7
4	8 8 9

3)

Stem	leaf
4	1 2
5	3 4 4 8
6	5 5 7 9

The Pie Graph or Circle Graph

1) red
2) 15%
3) black
4) 23%
5) 13%

Scatter Plots

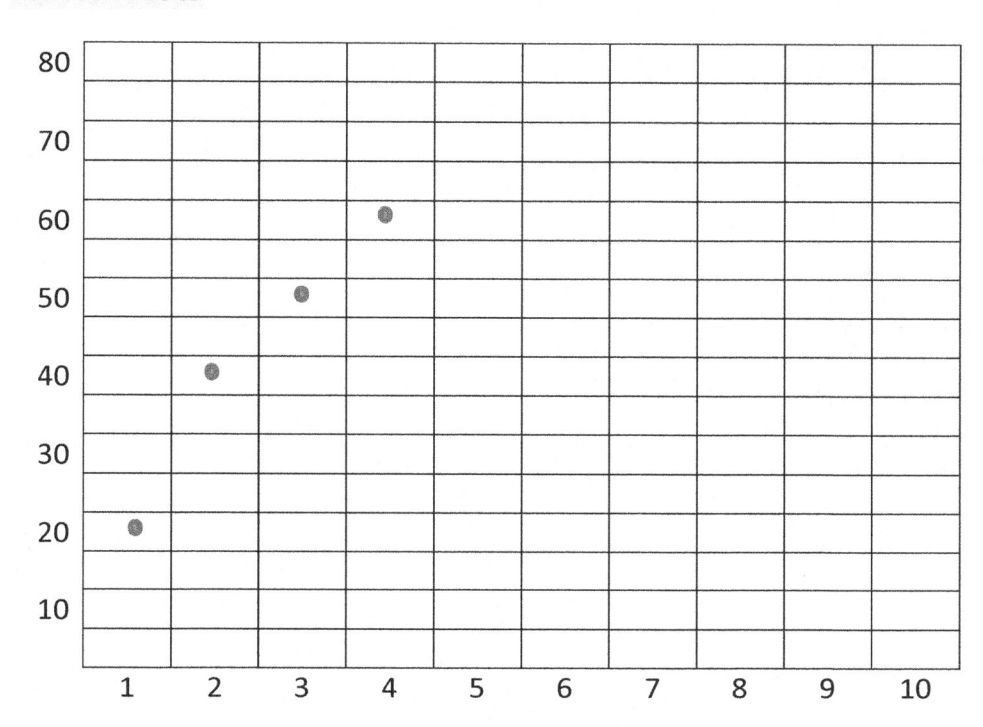

Probability Problems

1) $\frac{2}{5}$
2) $\frac{1}{10}$
3) $\frac{1}{5}$
4) $\frac{3}{10}$
5) $\frac{3}{10}$
6) $\frac{2}{5}$

ACCUPLACER Math in 7 Days

Day 6: Geometry

Math Topics that you'll learn today:

- ✓ The Pythagorean Theorem
- ✓ Area of Triangles
- ✓ Perimeter of Polygons
- ✓ Area and Circumference of Circles
- ✓ Area of Squares, Rectangles, and Parallelograms
- ✓ Area of Trapezoids
- ✓ Volume of Cubes
- ✓ Volume of Rectangle Prisms
- ✓ Surface Area of Cubes
- ✓ Surface Area of a Prism
- ✓ Volume of a Cylinder
- ✓ Surface Area of a Cylinder

Mathematics is, as it were, a sensuous logic, and relates to philosophy as do the arts, music, and plastic art to poetry. — K. Shegel

The Pythagorean Theorem

Helpful Hints

– In any right triangle:

$a^2 + b^2 = c^2$

Example:

Missing side = 5

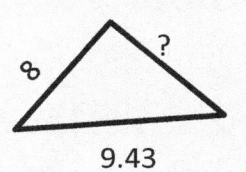

9.43

✎ Do the following lengths form a right triangle?

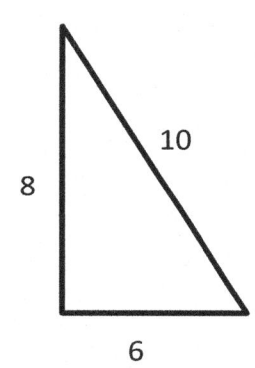

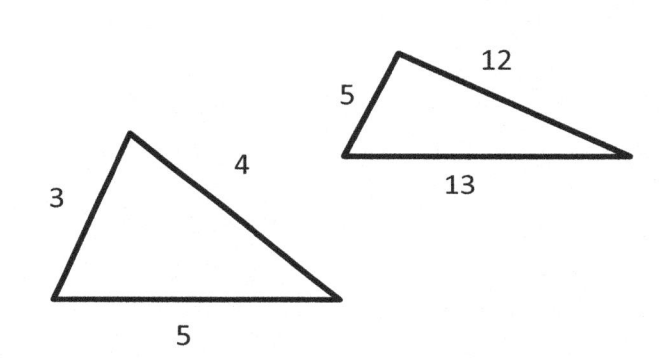

✎ Find each missing length to the nearest tenth.

4)

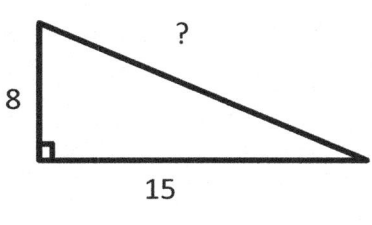

5)

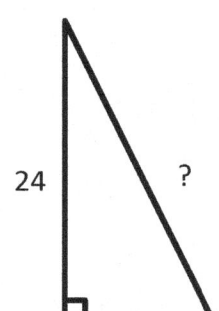

6)

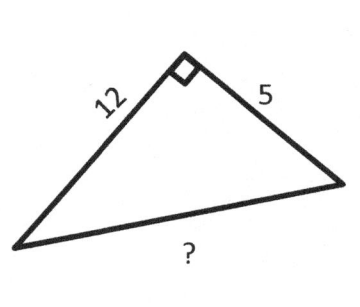

Area of Triangles

Helpful Hints

Area = $\frac{1}{2}$ (base × height)

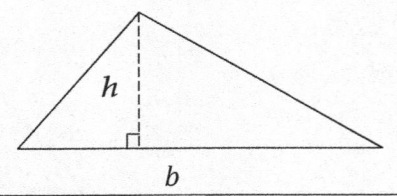

Find the area of each.

1)

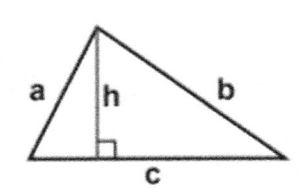

c = 9 mi
h = 3.7 mi

2)

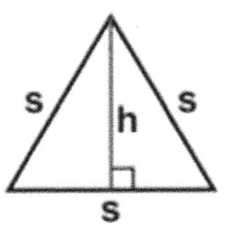

s = 14 m
h = 12.2 m

3)

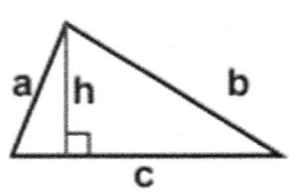

a = 5 m
b = 11 m
c = 14 m
h = 4 m

4)

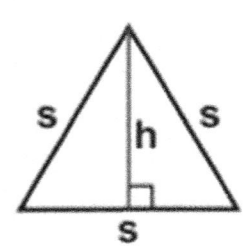

s = 10 m
h = 8.6 m

Perimeter of Polygons

Helpful Hints

Perimeter of a square = 4s

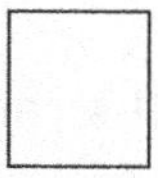

Perimeter of a rectangle = $2(l + w)$

Perimeter of trapezoid = a + b + c + d

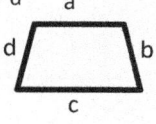

Perimeter of Pentagon = 6a

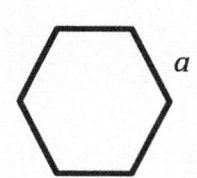

Perimeter of a parallelogram = $2(l + w)$

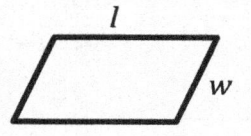

Example:

P = 18

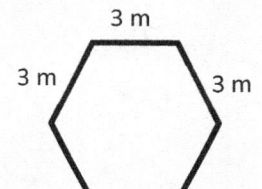

3 m, 3 m, 3 m

✏️ **Find the perimeter of each shape.**

1) Hexagon with sides 5 m, 5 m, 5 m

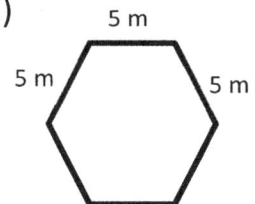

2) Parallelogram 15 mm, 15 mm, 15 mm, 15mm

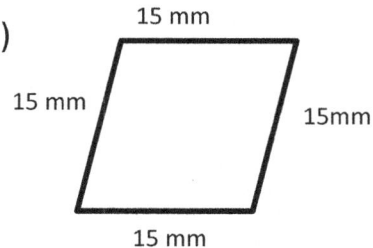

3) Rhombus 12 ft, 12 ft, 12 ft, 12 ft

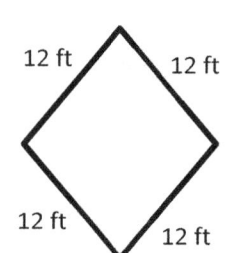

4) Rectangle 18 in, 12 in, 18 in, 12 in

www.EffortlessMath.com

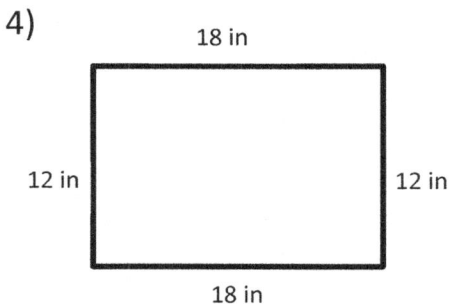

Area and Circumference of Circles

Helpful Hints

Area = πr²

Circumference = 2πr

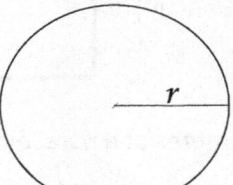

Example:

If the radius of a circle is 3, then:

Area = 28.27

Circumference = 18.85

✎ *Find the area and circumference of each.* (π = 3.14)

1) 4 in

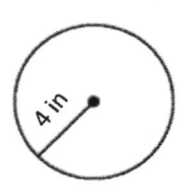

2) 18 cm

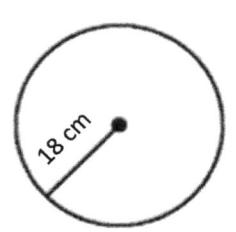

3) 5 m

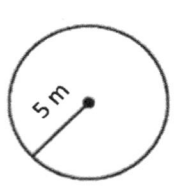

4) 11 cm

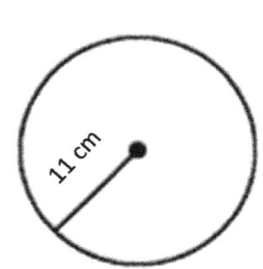

5) 8 km

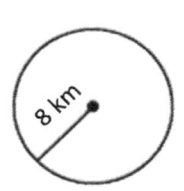

6) 21 in

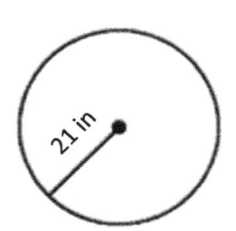

Area of Squares, Rectangles, and Parallelograms

Helpful Hints

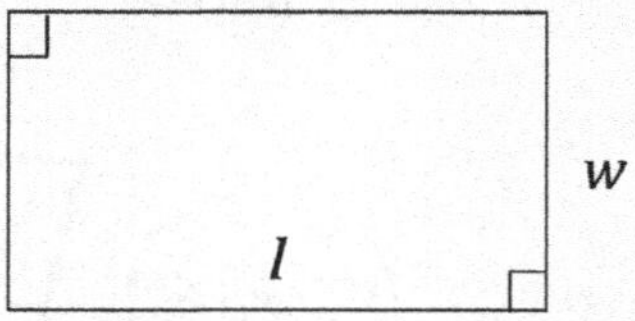

Area of Rectangles = Length × width

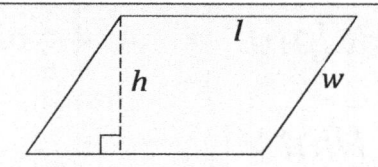

Area of Squares = s^2

Area of Parallelograms = length × height

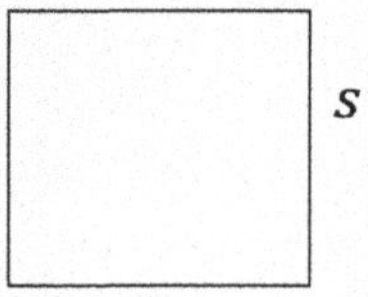

Example:

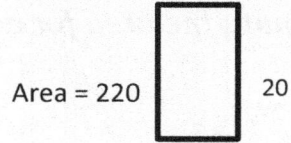

Area = 220

(rectangle 11 × 20)

✎ **Find the area of each.**

1) Rectangle: 22 yd × 32.3 yd

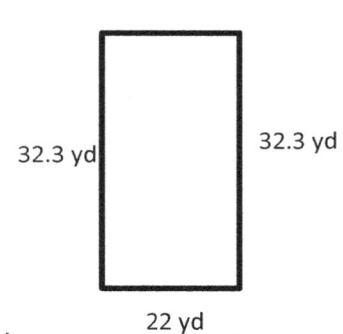

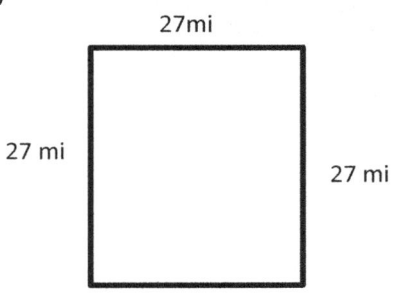

2) Square: 27 mi on each side

3) Parallelogram with sides 14.9 ft and 15.1 ft, height 7 ft

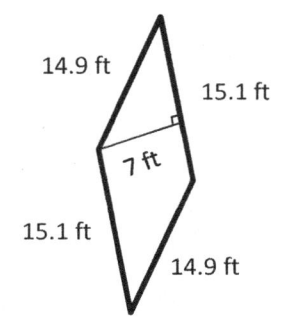

4) Parallelogram with base 5.9 in and height 4 in

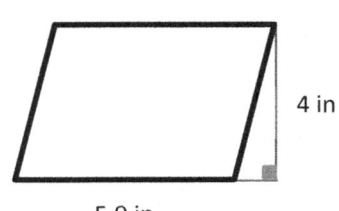

Area of Trapezoids

Helpful Hints

$A = \frac{1}{2}h(b_1 + b_2)$

Example:

$A = 252$ cm^2

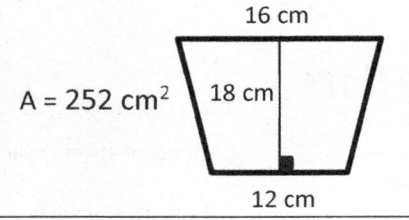

16 cm
18 cm
12 cm

✎ **Calculate the area for each trapezoid.**

1)

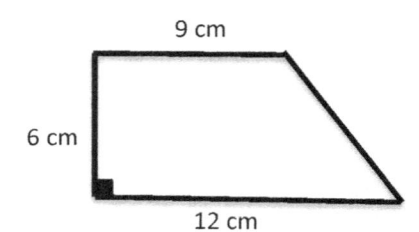

9 cm
6 cm
12 cm

2)

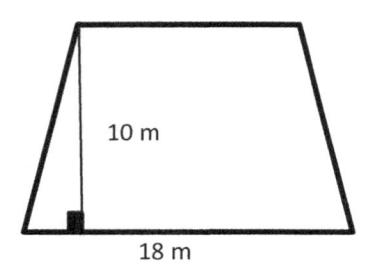

14 m
10 m
18 m

3)

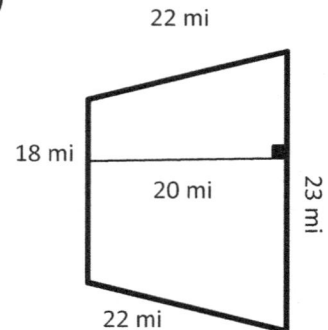

22 mi
18 mi
20 mi
23 mi
22 mi

4)

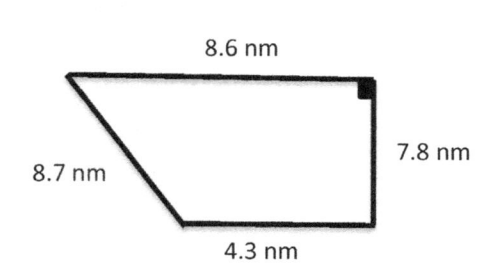

8.6 nm
8.7 nm
7.8 nm
4.3 nm

130

www.EffortlessMath.com

Volume of Cubes

Helpful Hints

– Volume is the measure of the amount of space inside of a solid figure, like a cube, ball, cylinder or pyramid.

– Volume of a cube = (one side)³

– Volume of a rectangle prism: Length × Width × Height

✎ Find the volume of each.

1)

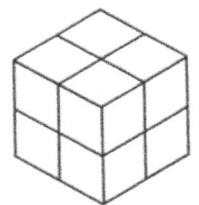

2)

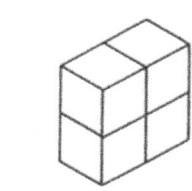

3)

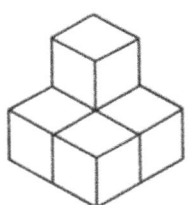

4)

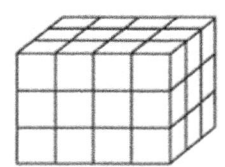

5)

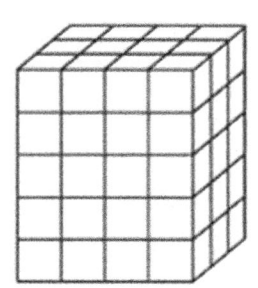

6)

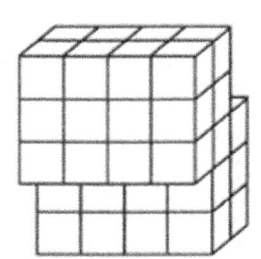

www.EffortlessMath.com

Volume of Rectangle Prisms

Helpful Hints

Volume of rectangle prism

length × width × height

Example:

10 × 5 × 8 = 400

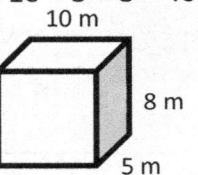

10 m
8 m
5 m

✎ Find the volume of each of the rectangular prisms.

1)

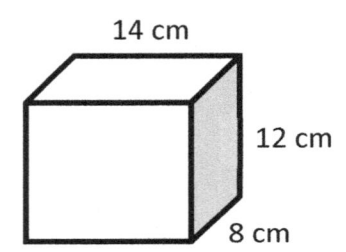

14 cm
12 cm
8 cm

2)

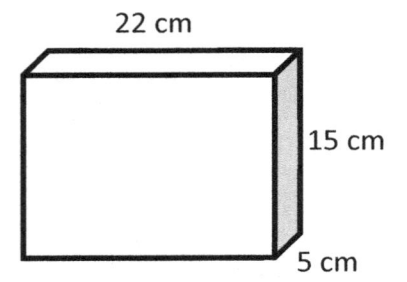

22 cm
15 cm
5 cm

3)

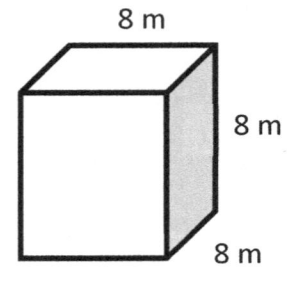

8 m
8 m
8 m

4)

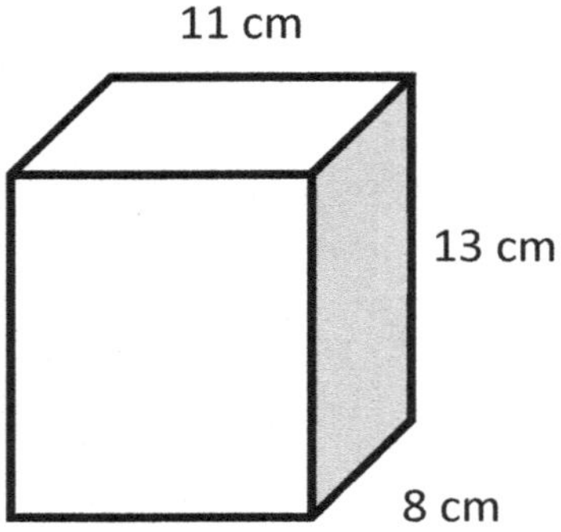

11 cm
13 cm
8 cm

132

www.EffortlessMath.com

Surface Area of Cubes

Helpful Hints

Surface Area of a cube =

6 × (one side of the cube)^2

Example:

6 × 4^2 = 96m^3

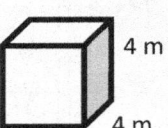

4 m
4 m
4 m

✏️ *Find the surface of each cube.*

1)

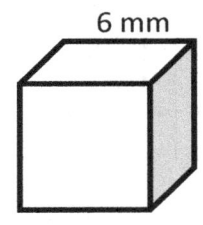

6 mm

2)

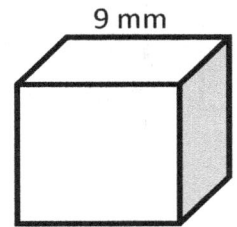

9 mm

3)

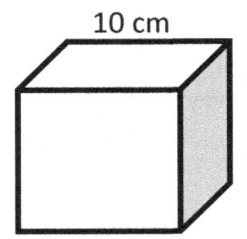

10 cm

4)

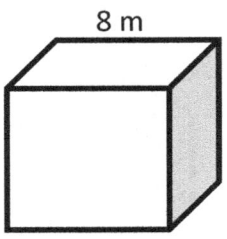

8 m

5)

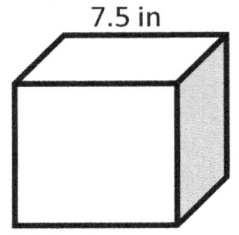

7.5 in

6)

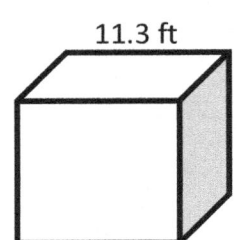

11.3 ft

Surface Area of a Rectangle Prism

> **Helpful Hints**
>
> Surface Area of a Rectangle Prism Formula:
>
> SA =2 [(width × length) + (height × length) + width × height)]

✎ **Find the surface of each prism.**

1) 3 yd, 6 yd, 10 yd

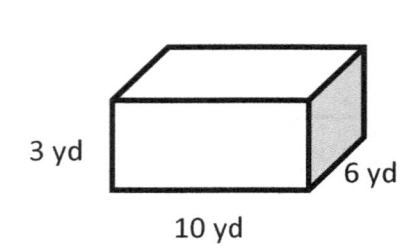

2) 7 mm, 7 mm, 7 mm

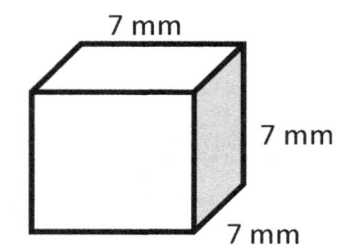

3) 8 in, 13.2 in, 6.7 in

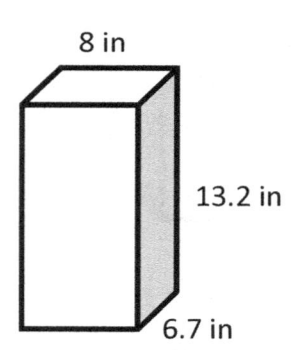

4) 17 cm, 17 cm, 11 cm

134

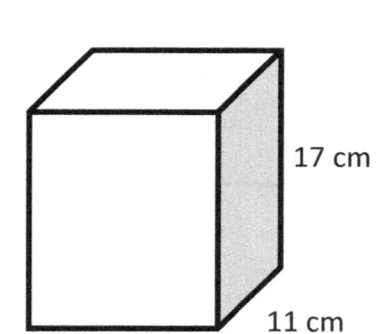

Volume of a Cylinder

Helpful Hints

Volume of Cylinder Formula = π(radius)² × height

π = 3.14

✎**Find the volume of each cylinder.** (π = 3.14)

1)

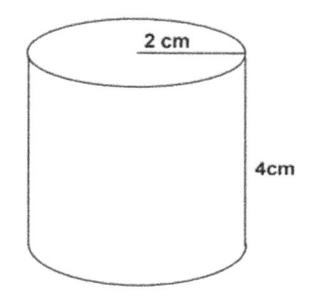

2 cm
4cm

2)

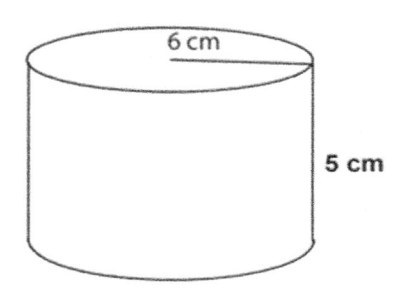

6 cm
5 cm

3)

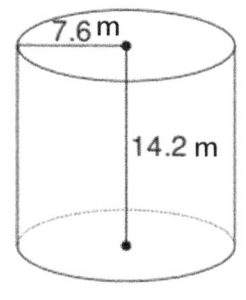

7.6 m
14.2 m

4)

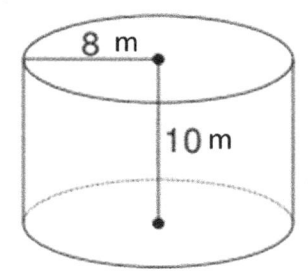

8 m
10 m

Surface Area of a Cylinder

Helpful Hints

Surface area of a cylinder

SA = 2πr² + 2πrh

Example:

Surface area

= 1727

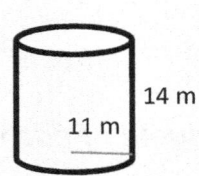

14 m
11 m

✎ **Find the surface of each cylinder.** (π = 3.14)

1)

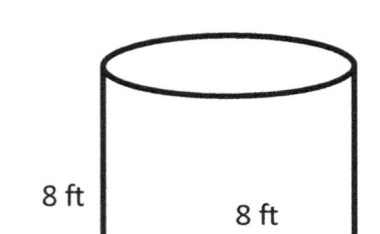

8 ft
8 ft

2)

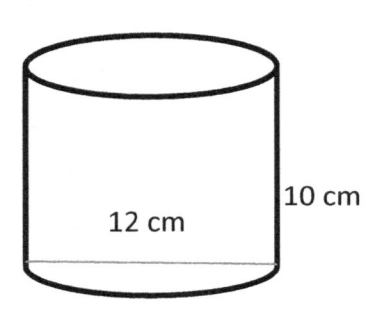

10 cm
12 cm

3)

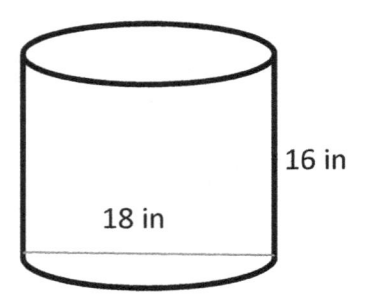

16 in
18 in

4)

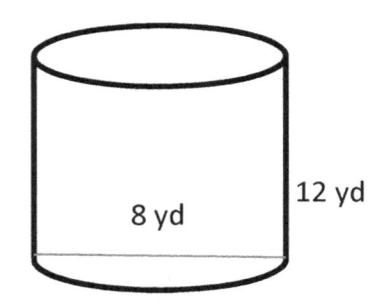

12 yd
8 yd

136   www.EffortlessMath.com

Answers of Worksheets – Day 7

The Pythagorean Theorem

1) yes
2) yes
3) yes
4) 17
5) 26
6) 13

Area of Triangles

1) 16.65 mi^2
2) 56 m^2
3) 85.4 m^2
4) 43 m^2

Perimeter of Polygons

1) 30 m
2) 60 mm
3) 48 ft
4) 60 in

Area and Circumference of Circles

1) Area: 50.24 in^2, Circumference: 25.12 in
2) Area: 1,017.36 cm^2, Circumference: 113.04 cm
3) Area: 78.5 m^2, Circumference: 31.4 m
4) Area: 379.94 cm^2, Circumference: 69.08 cm
5) Area: 200.96 km^2, Circumference: 50.2 km
6) Area: 1,384.74 km^2, Circumference: 131.88 km

Area of Squares, Rectangles, and Parallelograms

1) 710.6 yd^2
2) 729 mi^2
3) 105.7 ft^2
4) 23.6 in^2

Area of Trapezoids

1) 63 cm^2
2) 192 m^2
3) 451 mi^2
4) 50.31 nm^2

Volumes of Cubes

1) 8
2) 4
3) 5
4) 36
5) 60
6) 44

Volume of Rectangle Prisms

1) 1344 cm^3
2) 1650 cm^3
3) 512 m^3
4) 1144 cm^3

Surface Area of a Cube

1) 216 mm^2
2) 486 mm^2
3) 600 cm^2
4) 384 m^2
5) 337.5 in^2
6) 766.14 ft^2

Surface Area of a Prism

1) 216 yd^2
2) 294 mm^2
3) 495.28 in^2
4) 1326 cm^2

Volume of a Cylinder

1) 50.24 cm^3
2) 565.2 cm^3
3) 2,575.403 m^3
4) 2009.6 m^3

Surface Area of a Cylinder

1) 301.44 ft^2
2) 602.88 cm^2
3) 1413 in^2
4) 401.92 yd^2

Day 7: Geometry and Conic Sections

Math Topics that you'll learn today:

- ✓ Sketch Each Angle in Standard Position
- ✓ Finding Co–Terminal Angles and Reference Angles
- ✓ Writing Each Measure in Radians
- ✓ Writing Each Measure in Degrees
- ✓ Evaluating Each Trigonometric Expression
- ✓ Missing Sides and Angles of a Right Triangle
- ✓ Arc Length and Sector Area
- ✓ Trig Ratios of General Angles
- ✓ Finding the Focus, Vertex, and the Directrix of the Parabola
- ✓ Writing the Standard Form of the Circle
- ✓ Finding the Center and the Radius of Circles
- ✓ Arithmetic Sequences
- ✓ Geometric Sequences

"Wherever there is number, there is beauty." –Proclus

ACCUPLACER Math in 7 Days

Sketch Each Angle in Standard Position

Helpful Hints
- The standard position of an angle is when its vertex is located at the origin and its initial side extends along the positive x-axis.
- A positive angle is the angle measured in a counterclockwise direction from the initial side to the terminal side.
- A negative angle is the angle measured in a clockwise direction from the initial side to the terminal side.

✎ Draw the angle with the given measure in standard position.

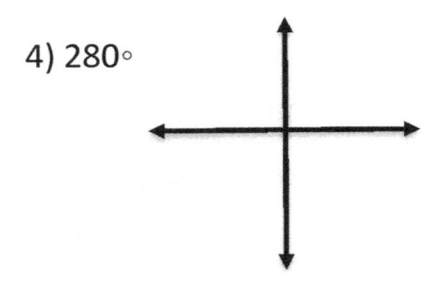

1) −120°

4) 280°

2) 440°

5) 710°

3) $-\dfrac{10\pi}{3}$

6) $\dfrac{11\pi}{6}$

140

www.EffortlessMath.com

Finding Co–Terminal Angles and Reference Angles

Helpful Hints
- Co-terminal angles are equal angles.
- To find a co-terminal of an angle, add or subtract 360 degrees (or 2π for radians) to the given angle.
- Reference angle is the smallest angle that you can make from the terminal side of an angle with the x-axis.

✎ Find a conterminal angle between 0° and 360°.

1) $-440°$

2) $640°$

3) $-435°$

4) $-330°$

✎ Find a conterminal angle between 0 and 2π for each given angle.

5) $\dfrac{15}{4}$

6) $-\dfrac{19}{12}$

7) $-\dfrac{35\pi}{18}$

8) $\dfrac{11\pi}{3}$

✎ Find the reference angle.

9)

10)

Writing Each Measure in Radians

Helpful Hints

$$radians = degrees \times \frac{\pi}{180}$$

Example:
Convert 150 degrees to radians.

$$radians = 150 \times \frac{\pi}{180} = \frac{5\pi}{6}$$

✎ **Convert each degree measure into radians.**

1) −140°

2) 320°

3) 210°

4) 970°

5) −190°

6) 345°

7) 265°

8) 555°

9) 300°

10) 50°

11) 315°

12) 600°

13) 712°

14) −160°

15) −210°

16) 545°

17) −30°

18) 660°

19) −170°

20) 230°

21) 150°

142

Writing Each Measure in Degrees

Helpful Hints

$$Degrees = radians \times \frac{180}{\pi}$$

Example: Convert $\frac{2\pi}{3}$ to degrees.
$\frac{2\pi}{3} \times \frac{180}{\pi} = \frac{360\pi}{3\pi} = 120$

✍ Convert each radian measure into degrees.

1) $\frac{\pi}{30}$

2) $\frac{32\pi}{40}$

3) $\frac{14\pi}{36}$

4) $\frac{\pi}{5}$

5) $-\frac{10\pi}{8}$

6) $\frac{14\pi}{3}$

7) $-\frac{16\pi}{3}$

8) $-\frac{50\pi}{14}$

9) $\frac{11\pi}{6}$

10) $\frac{5\pi}{9}$

11) $-\frac{\pi}{3}$

12) $\frac{13\pi}{6}$

13) $\frac{15\pi}{20}$

14) $\frac{21\pi}{4}$

15) $-\frac{68\pi}{45}$

16) $\frac{14\pi}{3}$

17) $-\frac{41\pi}{12}$

18) $-\frac{17\pi}{9}$

19) $\frac{35\pi}{18}$

20) $-\frac{3\pi}{2}$

21) $\frac{4\pi}{9}$

Evaluating Each Trigonometric

Helpful Hints
- Step 1: Draw the terminal side of the angle.
- Step 2: Find reference angle. (It is the smallest angle that you can make from the terminal side of an angle with the x-axis.)
- Step 3: Find the trigonometric function of the reference angle.

✎ *Find the exact value of each trigonometric function.*

1) $\cos 225°$

2) $\tan \dfrac{7\pi}{6}$

3) $\tan -\dfrac{\pi}{6}$

4) $\cot -\dfrac{7\pi}{6}$

5) $\cos -\dfrac{\pi}{4}$

6) $\cos -480°$

7) $\sin 690°$

8) $\tan 420°$

9) $\cot -495°$

10) $\tan 405°$

✎ *Use the given point on the terminal side of angle θ to find the value of the trigonometric function indicated.*

11) $\sin \theta;\ (-6, 4)$

12) $\cos \theta;\ (2, -2)$

13) $\cot \theta;\ (-7, \sqrt{15})$

14) $\cos \theta;\ (-2\sqrt{3}, -2)$

15) $\sin \theta;\ (-\sqrt{7}, 3)$

16) $\tan \theta;\ (-11, -2)$

Missing Sides and Angles of a Right Triangle

Helpful Hints

SOH – CAH - TOA

$sine\ \theta = \frac{opposite}{hypotenus}$, $Cos\ \theta = \frac{adjacent}{hypotenuse}$, $\tan \theta = \frac{opposite}{adjacent}$

✏ Find the value of each trigonometric ratio as fractions in their simplest form.

1) tan A

2) sin X

✏ Find the missing side. Round answers to the nearest tenth.

3)

4)

5)

6)

Arc Length and Sector Area

✏️ **Find the length of each arc. Round your answers to the nearest tenth.**

Helpful	Area of a sector $= \frac{1}{2}r^2\theta$
Hints	length of a sector $= (\frac{\theta}{180})\pi r$

1) r = 28 cm, θ = 45°

3) r = 22 ft, θ = 60°

2) r = 15 ft, θ = 95°

4) r = 12 m, θ = 85°

✏️ **Find area of a sector. Do not round.**

5)

7)

6)

8)

Trig Ratios of General Angles

✎ Use a calculator to find each. Round your answers to the nearest ten–

Helpful Hints

θ	0°	30°	45°	60°	90°
sin θ	0	$\frac{1}{2}$	$\frac{\sqrt{2}}{2}$	$\frac{\sqrt{3}}{2}$	1
cos θ	1	$\frac{\sqrt{3}}{2}$	$\frac{\sqrt{2}}{2}$	$\frac{1}{2}$	0
tan θ	0	$\frac{\sqrt{3}}{3}$	1	$\sqrt{3}$	undefined

thousandth.

1) sin − 120°

2) sin − 228°

3) cos 310°

4) cos 101°

5) sin 105°

6) sin − 305°

✎ Find the exact value of each trigonometric function. Some may be undefined.

7) sec 0

8) tan $-\frac{3\pi}{2}$

9) cos $\frac{11}{6}$

10) cot $\frac{5\pi}{3}$

11) sec $-\frac{3\pi}{4}$

12) tan $\frac{2\pi}{3}$

Finding the Focus, Vertex, and Directrix of a Parabola

> **Helpful Hints**
>
> Parabola:
> When it opens up or down:
> $(x + h)^2 = 4p(y - k)$, Vertex: (h, k), Directrix: $y = k - p$
> Focus: $(h, k + p)$
> When it opens right or left:
> $(y + k)^2 = 4p(x - h)$, Vertex: (h, k), Directrix: $x = h - p$
> Focus: $(h + p, k)$

✎ *Use the information provided to write the vertex form equation of each parabola.*

1) $y = x^2 + 8x$

2) $y = x^2 - 6x + 5$

3) $y + 6 = (x + 3)^2$

4) $y = x^2 + 10x + 33$

5) $y = (x + 5)(x + 4)$

6) $\frac{1}{2}(y + 4) = (x - 7)^2$

7) $162 + 731 = -y - 9x^2$

8) $y = x^2 + 16x + 71$

9) Focus: $(-\frac{63}{8}, -7)$, Directrix: $x = -\frac{65}{8}$

10) Focus: $(\frac{107}{12}, -7)$, Directrix: $x = \frac{109}{12}$

11) Opens up or down, and passes through (−6, −7), (−11, −2), and (−8, 1)

12) Opens up or down, and passes through (11, 15), (7, 7), and (4, 22)

Writing the Standard Form of a Circle

Helpful Hints

Equation of circles in standard form:
$(x - h)^2 + (y - k)^2 = r^2$
Center: (h, k), Radius: r

General format: $ax^2 + by^2 + cx + dy + e = 0$

✎ Use the information provided to write the standard form equation of each circle.

1) $x^2 + y^2 - 8x - 6y + 21 = 0$

2) $y^2 + 2x + x^2 = 24y - 120$

3) $x^2 + y^2 - 2y - 15 = 0$

4) $8x + x^2 - 2y = 64 - y^2$

5) Center: (−5, −6), Radius: 9

6) Center: (−9, −12), Radius: 4

7) Center: (−12, −5), Area: 4π

8) Center: (−11, −14), Area: 16π

9) Center: (−3, 2), Circumference: 2π

10) Center: (15, 14), Circumference: $2\pi\sqrt{15}$

ACCUPLACER Math in 7 Days

Finding the Center and the Radius of Circles

Helpful Hints

$(x - h)^2 + (y - k)^2 = r^2$

center: (h, k), radius: r

✍ *Identify the center and radius of each. Then sketch the graph.*

1) $()^2 + ()^2 = 10$

   $x - 2 \qquad y + 5$

2) $^2 + ()^2 = 4$

   $x \qquad y - 1$

3) $()^2 + ()^2 = 9$

   $x - 2 \qquad y + 6$

4) $()^2 + ()^2 = 16$

   $x + 14 \qquad y - 5$

150

www.EffortlessMath.com

Arithmetic Sequences

Helpful Hints

$x_n = a + d(n - 1)$

a = the first term
d = the common difference between terms
n = how many terms to add up

✍ Given the first term and the common difference of an arithmetic sequence find the first five terms and the explicit formula.

1) $a_1 = 24$, $d = 2$

2) $a_1 = -15$, $d = -5$

3) $a_1 = 18$, $d = 10$

4) $a_1 = -38$, $d = -100$

✍ Given a term in an arithmetic sequence and the common difference find the first five terms and the explicit formula.

5) $a_{36} = -276$, $d = -7$

6) $a_{37} = 249$, $d = 8$

7) $a_{38} = -53.2$, $d = -1.1$

8) $a_{40} = -1191$, $d = -30$

✍ Given a term in an arithmetic sequence and the common difference find the recursive formula and the three terms in the sequence after the last one given.

9) $a_{22} = -44$, $d = -2$

10) $a_{12} = 28.6$, $d = 1.8$

11) $a_{18} = 27.4$, $d = 1.1$

12) $a_{21} = -1.4$, $d = 0.6$

Geometric Sequences

Helpful Hints

$x_n = ar^{(n-1)}$

a = the first term
r = the common ratio

✎ *Determine if the sequence is geometric. If it is, find the common ratio.*

1) $1, -5, 25, -125, \ldots$

2) $-2, -4, -8, -16, \ldots$

3) $4, 16, 36, 64, \ldots$

4) $-3, -15, -75, -375, \ldots$

✎ *Given the first term and the common ratio of a geometric sequence find the first five terms and the explicit formula.*

5) $a_1 = 0.8, r = -5$

6) $a_1 = 1, r = 2$

✎ *Given the recursive formula for a geometric sequence find the common ratio, the first five terms, and the explicit formula.*

7) $a_n = a_{n-1} \cdot 2, a_1 = 2$

8) $a_n = a_{n-1} \cdot -3, a_1 = -3$

9) $a_n = a_{n-1} \cdot 5, a_1 = 2$

10) $a_n = a_{n-1} \cdot 3, a_1 = -3$

✎ *Given two terms in a geometric sequence find the 8th term and the recursive formula.*

11) $a_4 = 12$ and $a_5 = -6$

12) $a_5 = 768$ and $a_2 = 12$

Answers of Worksheets – Day 7

Sketch each angle in standard position

1) −120°

2) 440°

3) −$\frac{10\pi}{3}$

4) 280°

5) 710°

6) $\frac{11\pi}{6}$

Finding co–terminal angles and reference angles

1) 280°
2) 280°
3) 285°
4) 30°

5) $\frac{7\pi}{4}$
6) $\frac{5\pi}{12}$
7) $\frac{\pi}{18}$

8) $\frac{5\pi}{3}$
9) $\frac{2\pi}{9}$
10) 80°

Writing each measure in radians

1) $-\frac{7\pi}{9}$
2) $\frac{16\pi}{9}$
3) $\frac{7\pi}{6}$
4) $\frac{97}{18}$
5) $-\frac{19}{18}$
6) $\frac{23}{12}$
7) $\frac{53}{36}$

8) $\frac{37}{12}$
9) $\frac{5\pi}{3}$
10) $\frac{5\pi}{18}$
11) $\frac{7\pi}{4}$
12) $\frac{10}{3}$
13) $\frac{178\pi}{45}$
14) $-\frac{8\pi}{9}$

15) $-\frac{7\pi}{6}$
16) $\frac{109\pi}{36}$
17) $-\frac{\pi}{6}$
18) $\frac{11\pi}{3}$
19) $-\frac{17\pi}{18}$
20) $\frac{23\pi}{18}$
21) $\frac{5\pi}{6}$

Writing each measure in degrees

1) $6°$
2) $144°$
3) $70°$
4) $36°$
5) $-225°$
6) $840°$
7) $-960°$

8) $-643°$
9) $330°$
10) $100°$
11) $-60°$
12) $390°$
13) $135°$
14) $945°$

15) $-272°$
16) $840°$
17) $-615°$
18) $-340°$
19) $350°$
20) $-270°$
21) $80°$

Evaluating each trigonometric expression

1) $-\frac{\sqrt{2}}{2}$
2) $\frac{\sqrt{3}}{3}$
3) $-\frac{\sqrt{3}}{3}$
4) $-\sqrt{3}$
5) $\frac{\sqrt{2}}{2}$

6) $-\frac{1}{2}$
7) $-\frac{1}{2}$
8) $\sqrt{3}$
9) 1
10) 1
11) $\frac{2\sqrt{13}}{13}$

12) $-\sqrt{2}$
13) $-\frac{7\sqrt{15}}{15}$
14) $-\frac{\sqrt{3}}{2}$
15) $\frac{3}{4}$
16) $\frac{2}{11}$

Missing sides and angles of a right triangle

1) $\frac{4}{3}$
2) $\frac{3}{5}$
3) 31.4
4) 7.0
5) 16.2
6) 31.1

Arc length and sector area

1) 22 cm
2) 25 ft
3) 23 ft
4) 18 m
5) 114π ft^2
6) $\frac{343\pi}{2}$ in^2
7) 147π cm^2
8) $\frac{512\pi}{3}$ ft^2

Trig ratios of general angles

1) -0.8660
2) 0.7431
3) 0.6428
4) -0.1908
5) 0.9659
6) 0.8192
7) 1
8) Undefined
9) $\frac{\sqrt{3}}{2}$
10) $-\frac{\sqrt{3}}{3}$
11) $-\sqrt{2}$
12) $-\sqrt{3}$

Finding the Focus, Vertex, and the Directrix of a Parabola

1) $y = (x + 4)^2 - 16$
2) $y = (x - 3)^2 - 4$
3) $y = (x + 3)^2 - 6$
4) $y = (x + 5)^2 + 8$
5) $y = (x + \frac{9}{2})^2 - \frac{1}{4}$
6) $y = 2(x - 7)^2 - 4$
7) $y = -9(x + 9)^2 - 2$
8) $y = (x + 8)^2 + 7$
9) $x = 2(y + 7)^2 - 8$
10) $x = -3(y + 7)^2 + 9$
11) $y = -(x + 9)^2 + 2$
12) $y = (x - 8)^2 + 6$

Writing the Standard Form of a Circle

1) $(x - 4)^2 + (y - 3)^2 = 4$
2) $(x + 1)^2 + (y - 12)^2 = 25$
3) $x^2 + (y - 1)^2 = 16$
4) $(x + 4)^2 + (y - 1)^2 = 81$
5) $(x + 5)^2 + (y + 6)^2 = 81$
6) $(x + 9)^2 + (y + 12)^2 = 16$

7) $(x + 12)^2 + (y + 5)^2 = 4$

8) $(x + 11)^2 + (y + 14)^2 = 16$

9) $(x + 3)^2 + (y - 2)^2 = 1$

10) $(x - 15)^2 + (y - 14)^2 = 15$

Finding the Center and the Radius of Circles

1) Center: (2, −5), Radius: $\sqrt{10}$

2) Center: (0, 1), Radius: $2\sqrt{26}$

3) Center: (2, −6), Radius: 3

4) Center: (−14, −5), Radius: 4

Arithmetic Sequences

1) First Five Terms: 24, 26, 28, 30, 32, Explicit: $a_n = 22 + 2n$
2) First Five Terms: −15, −20, −25, −30, −35, Explicit: $a_n = -10 - 5n$
3) First Five Terms: 18, 28, 38, 48, 58, Explicit: $a_n = 8 + 10n$
4) First Five Terms: −38, −138, −238, −338, −438, Explicit: $a_n = 62 - 100n$
5) First Five Terms: −31, −38, −45, −52, −59, Explicit: $a_n = -24 - 7n$
6) First Five Terms: −39, −31, −23, −15, −7, Explicit: $a_n = -47 + 8n$
7) First Five Terms: −12.5, −13.6, −14.7, −15.8, −16.9, Explicit: $a_n = -11.4 - 1.1n$
8) First Five Terms: −21, −51, −81, −111, −141, Explicit: $a_n = 9 - 30n$
9) Next 3 terms: −46, −48, −50, Recursive: $a_n = a_{n-1} - 2$, $a_1 = -2$
10) Next 3 terms: 30.4, 32.2, 34, Recursive: $a_n = a_{n-1} + 1.8$, $a_1 = 8.8$
11) Next 3 terms: 28.5, 29.6, 30.7, Recursive: $a_n = a_{n-1} + 1.1$, $a_1 = 8.7$
12) Next 3 terms: −0.8, −0.2, 0.4, Recursive: $a_n = a_{n-1} + 0.6$, $a_1 = -13.4$

Geometric Sequences

1) $r = -5$
2) $r = 2$
3) not geometric
4) $r = 5$
5) First Five Terms: 0.8, −4, 20, −100, 500

    Explicit: $a_n = 0.8 \cdot (-5)^{n-1}$

6) First Five Terms: 1, 2, 4, 8, 16

    Explicit: $a_n = 2^{n-1}$

7) Common Ratio: $r = 2$

    First Five Terms: 2, 4, 8, 16. 32

    Explicit: $a_n = 2 \cdot 2^{n-1}$

8) Common Ratio: $r = -3$

    First Five Terms: −3, 9, −27, 81, −243

    Explicit: $a_n = -3 \cdot (-3)^{n-1}$

9) Common Ratio: $r = 5$

    First Five Terms: 2, 10, 50, 250, 1250

    Explicit: $a_n = 2 \cdot 5^{n-1}$

10) Common Ratio: r = 3

    First Five Terms: $-3, -9, -27, -81, -243$

    Explicit: $a_n = -3 \cdot 3^{n-1}$

11) $a_8 = \dfrac{3}{4}$, Recursive: $a_n = a_{n-1} \cdot \dfrac{-1}{2}$, $a_1 = -96$

12) $a_8 = 49152$, Recursive: $a_n = a_{n-1} \cdot 4$, $a_1 = 3$

ACCUPLACER Mathematics Practice Tests

According to College Board website all ACCUPLACER tests use a multiple-choice format and there's no time limit on the tests, so you can focus on doing your best to demonstrate your skills.

ACCUPLACER uses the computer-adaptive technology and the questions you see are based on your skill level. Your response to each question drives the difficulty level of the next question.

The number of questions varies depending on which ACCUPLACER tests you take. There could be as few as 12 questions or as many as 40.

There are three Math sections on ACCUPLACER test.

Arithmetic

The Arithmetic test measures your ability to perform basic arithmetic operations and to solve problems that involve fundamental arithmetic concepts.

Elementary Algebra

The Elementary Algebra test measures your ability to perform basic algebraic operations and to solve problems involving elementary algebraic concepts.

College-Level Math

The College-Level Math test measures your ability to solve problems that involve college-level mathematics concepts.

ACCUPLACER does NOT permit the use of personal calculators on the Math portion of placement test. ACCUPLACER expects students to be able to answer certain questions without the assistance of a calculator. Therefore, they provide an onscreen calculator for students to use on some questions.

In this section, there are two complete ACCUPLACER Mathematics Tests.

Take these tests to see what score you'll be able to receive on a real ACCUPLACER test.

Good luck!

Time to Test

Time to refine your skill with a practice examination

Take practice ACCUPLACER Math Tests to simulate the test day experience. After you've finished, score your test using the answer keys.

Before You Start

- You'll need a pencil and scratch papers to take the test.
- For these practice tests, don't time yourself. Spend time as much as you need.
- It's okay to guess. You won't lose any points if you're wrong.
- After you've finished the test, review the answer key to see where you went wrong.

Mathematics is like love; a simple idea, but it can get complicated.

ACCUPLACER Mathematics Practice Test 1

(Non–Calculator)

2 Sections – 40 questions

Total time for two sections: No Time Limit

You may not use a calculator on this section.

Arithmetic and Elementary Algebra

1) $(x + 7)(x + 5) =$

   A. $x^2 + 12x + 12$

   B. $2x + 12x + 12$

   C. $x^2 + 35x + 12$

   D. $x^2 + 12x + 35$

2) If x is a positive integer divisible by 6, and $x < 60$, what is the greatest possible value of x?

   A. 54

   B. 48

   C. 36

   D. 59

3) $x^2 - 81 = 0$, x could equal to:

   A. 6

   B. 9

   C. 12

   D. 15

4) If a = 8, what is the value of b in this equation?

$$b = \frac{a^2}{4} + 4$$

    A. 24

    B. 22

    C. 20

    D. 28

5) If $6.5 < x \leq 9.0$, then x cannot be equal to:

    A. 6.5

    B. 9

    C. 7.2

    D. 7.5

6) What is the area of an isosceles right triangle that has one leg that measures 6 cm?

    A. 18 cm

    B. 36 cm

    C. $6\sqrt{2}$ cm

    D. 72 cm

7) Which of the following expressions is equivalent to $10 - \frac{2}{3}x \geq 12$

   A. $x \geq -3$

   B. $x \leq -3$

   C. $x \geq 24\frac{1}{3}$

   D. $x \leq 24\frac{1}{3}$

8) Which of the following is a factor of both $x^2 - 2x - 8$ and $x^2 - 6x + 8$?

   A. $(x - 4)$

   B. $(x + 4)$

   C. $(x - 2)$

   D. $(x + 2)$

9) $\frac{1}{6b^2} + \frac{1}{6b} = \frac{1}{b^2}$, then $b = ?$

   A. $-\frac{16}{15}$

   B. 5

   C. $-\frac{15}{16}$

   D. 8

10) If two angles in a triangle measure 53 degrees and 45 degrees, what is the value of the third angle?

   A. 8 degrees

   B. 42 degrees

   C. 82 degrees

   D. 98 degrees

11) A soccer team played 120 games and won 70 percent of them. How many games did the team win?

   A. 84

   B. 94

   C. 104

   D. 114

12) Line m passes through the point (−1, 2). Which of the following CANNOT be the equation of line m?

   A. $y = 1 - x$

   B. $y = x + 1$

   C. $x = -1$

   D. $y = x + 3$

13) $(p^4) \cdot (p^5) =$ ___

   A. P^{20}

   B. $2P^9$

   C. P^9

   D. $2P^{20}$

14) If a = 8 what's the value of $4a^2 + 3a + 10$?

   A. 166

   B. 216

   C. 290

   D. 276

15) If $a^5 + b^5 = a^5 + c^5$, then b = ?

   A. c

   B. a

   C. $b^4 - a^4$

   D. $a^4 - b^4$

16) The equation of a line is given as: $y = 5x - 3$. Which of the following points does not lie on the line?

    A. (1, 2)

    B. (−2, −13)

    C. (3, 18)

    D. (2, 7)

17) $5^{\frac{7}{3}} \times 5^{\frac{2}{3}} =$

    A. 5^2

    B. 5^1

    C. 5^3

    D. 3^0

18) What is 152.6588 rounded to the nearest hundredth?

    A. 152.65

    B. 152.66

    C. 153

    D. 152.659

19) The sum of three numbers is 45. If another number is added to these three numbers, the average of the four numbers is 20.

What is the fourth number?

A. 20

B. 35

C. 40

D. 45

20) David owed $8240. After making 45 payments of $124 each, how much did he have left to pay?

A. $2660

B. $3660

C. $5580

D. $6800

College–Level Mathematics

1) If f(x) = 5 + x and g(x) = $-x^2 - 1 - 2x$, then find (g − f)(x)?

   A. $x^2 - 3x - 6$

   B. $x^2 - 3x + 6$

   C. $-x^2 - 3x + 6$

   D. $-x^2 - 3x - 6$

2) $\frac{|3+x|}{7} \leq 5$, then x = ?

   A. $-38 \leq x \leq 35$

   B. $-38 \leq x \leq 32$

   C. $-32 \leq x \leq 38$

   D. $-32 \leq x \leq 32$

3) $\tan\left(-\frac{\pi}{6}\right)$ = ?

   A. $\frac{\sqrt{3}}{3}$

   B. $-\frac{\sqrt{2}}{2}$

   C. $\frac{\sqrt{2}}{2}$

   D. $-\frac{\sqrt{3}}{3}$

4) $\frac{\sqrt{32a^5b^3}}{\sqrt{2ab^2}} = ?$

   A. $4a^2 \sqrt{b}$

   B. $2b^2 \sqrt{a}$

   C. $4b^2 \sqrt{a}$

   D. $-4a^2 \sqrt{b}$

5) The cost, in thousands of dollars, of producing x thousands of textbooks is $C(x) = x^2 + 10x + 30$. The revenue, also in thousands of dollars, is $R(x) = 4x$. Find the profit or loss if 3,000 textbooks are produced. (profit = revenue − cost)

   A. $21,000 loss

   B. $57,000 profit

   C. $3,000 profit

   D. $57,000 loss

6) Suppose a triangle has the dimensions indicated below:

   Then Sin B = ?

   A. $\frac{3}{5}$

   B. $\frac{4}{5}$

   C. $\frac{4}{3}$

   D. $\frac{3}{4}$

7) Find the slope–intercept form of the graph $6x - 7y = -12$

A. $y = -\frac{7}{6}x - \frac{12}{7}$

B. $y = -\frac{6}{7}x + 12$

C. $y = \frac{6}{7}x + \frac{12}{7}$

D. $y = \frac{7}{6}x - 12$

8) Ella (E) is 4 years older than her friend Ava (A) who is 3 years younger than her sister Sofia (S). If E, A and S denote their ages, which one of the following represents the given information?

A. $\begin{cases} E = A + 4 \\ S = A - 3 \end{cases}$

B. $\begin{cases} E = A + 4 \\ A = S + 3 \end{cases}$

C. $\begin{cases} A = E + 4 \\ S = A - 3 \end{cases}$

D. $\begin{cases} E = A + 4 \\ A = S - 3 \end{cases}$

9) Which of the following point is the solution of the system of equations?

$$\begin{cases} 5x + y = 9 \\ 10x - 7y = -18 \end{cases}$$

A. (2, 4)

B. (2, 2)

C. (1, 4)

D. (0, 4)

10) Find the Center and Radius of the graph $(x - 3)^2 + (y + 6)^2 = 12$

A. (3, 6), $\sqrt{3}$

B. (3, −6), $2\sqrt{3}$

C. (−3, 6), $2\sqrt{3}$

D. (3, −6), $\sqrt{3}$

11) Simplify $\dfrac{4 - 3i}{-4i}$

A. $\dfrac{3}{4} + i$

B. $\dfrac{3}{4} - i$

C. $\dfrac{1}{4} - i$

D. $\dfrac{1}{4} + i$

12) What is the domain of the following function?

$$f(x) = \sqrt{x-2} + 5$$

    A. $x \leq 2$

    B. $x > 2$

    C. $x \geq 2$

    D. $x > 2$

13) Find the inverse function of $f(x) = \dfrac{x-2}{6}$

    A. $\dfrac{1}{3}(x+3)$

    B. $x + 3$

    C. $2(3x+1)$

    D. $3x + 1$

14) A number is chosen at random from 1 to 25. Find the probability of not selecting a composite number.

    A. $\dfrac{1}{25}$

    B. 25

    C. $\dfrac{2}{5}$

    D. 1

15) Solve $e^{x-2} = 20$

A. ln (20) + 2

B. 2 − ln (20)

C. ln (2) + 20

D. ln (2) − 20

16) Solve the equation: $\log_2(x+3) - \log_2(x-1) = 1$

A. 3

B. 1

C. 0

D. 5

17) If $\tan \theta = \frac{5}{12}$ and $\sin \theta > 0$, then $\cos \theta = ?$

A. $-\frac{5}{13}$

B. $\frac{12}{13}$

C. $\frac{13}{12}$

D. $-\frac{12}{13}$

18) From 8 students in an algebra class, a group of 3 students will be chosen to work on a group project. How many different groups of 3 students can be chosen?

   A. 3

   B. 8

   C. 56

   D. 60

19) If $f(x) = \frac{6x-2}{3}$ and $f^{-1}(x)$, is the inverse of f(x), what is the value of $f^{-1}(2)$?

   A. $\frac{4}{3}$

   B. $\frac{12}{5}$

   C. $\frac{3}{4}$

   D. $\frac{5}{12}$

20) Which of the following lines is parallel to the graph of $y = 2x$?

   A. $4x - y = 4$

   B. $2x - 2y = 2$

   C. $2x - y = 4$

   D. $2x + y = 2$

ACCUPLACER Mathematics Practice Test 2

(Non–Calculator)

2 Sections – 40 questions

Total time for two sections: No Time Limit

You may not use a calculator on this section.

Arithmetic and Elementary Algebra

1) $(x - 4)(x^2 + 5x + 4) = ?$

   A. $x^3 + x^2 - 16x + 16$

   B. $x^3 + 2x^2 - 16x - 16$

   C. $x^3 + x^2 - 16x - 16$

   D. $x^3 + x^2 + 16x - 15$

2) How many 3 × 3 squares can fit inside a rectangle with a height of 54 and width of 12?

   A. 72

   B. 52

   C. 62

   D. 42

3) If $7 + 2x \leq 15$, what is the value of $x \leq$?

   A. $14x$

   B. 4

   C. -4

   D. $15x$

4) Liam's average (arithmetic mean) on two mathematics tests is 8. What should Liam's score be on the next test to have an overall of 9 for all the tests?

   A. 8

   B. 9

   C. 10

   D. 11

5) $7^7 \times 7^8 = ?$

   A. 7^{56}

   B. $7^{0.89}$

   C. 7^{15}

   D. 1^7

6) What is 5231.48245 rounded to the nearest tenth?

   A. 5231.482

   B. 5231.5

   C. 5231

   D. 5231.48

7) 15 is what percent of 75?

   A. 10%

   B. 20%

   C. 30%

   D. 40%

8) Last Friday Jacob had $32.52. Over the weekend he received some money for cleaning the attic. He now has $44. How much money did he receive?

   A. $76.52

   B. $11.48

   C. $32.08

   D. $12.58

9) Simplify $\dfrac{\frac{1}{2} - \frac{x+5}{4}}{\frac{x^2}{2} - \frac{5}{2}}$

   A. $\dfrac{3-x}{x^2-10}$

   B. $\dfrac{3-x}{2x^2-10}$

   C. $\dfrac{3+x}{x^2-10}$

   D. $\dfrac{-3-x}{2x^2-10}$

10) $\sqrt{47}$ is between which two whole numbers?

   A. 3 and 4

   B. 4 and 5

   C. 5 and 6

   D. 6 and 7

11) A man owed $4265 on his car. After making 55 payment of $77 each, how much did he have left to pay?

   A. $4235

   B. $300

   C. $4164

   D. $30

12) Find all values of x for which $4x^2 + 14x + 6 = 0$

   A. $-\frac{3}{2}, -\frac{1}{2}$

   B. $-\frac{1}{2}, -3$

   C. $-2, -\frac{1}{3}$

   D. $-\frac{2}{3}, \frac{1}{2}$

13) $(x^6)^{\frac{5}{8}}$

A. $x^{\frac{4}{15}}$

B. $x^{\frac{53}{8}}$

C. $x^{\frac{15}{4}}$

D. $x^{\frac{8}{53}}$

14) If a vehicle is driven 32 miles on Monday, 35 miles on Tuesday, and 29 miles on Wednesday, what is the average number of miles driven each day?

A. 32 miles

B. 31 miles

C. 29 miles

D. 33 miles

15) In the following diagram what is the value of x in the following triangle?

A. 60°

B. 90°

C. 45°

D. 15°

16) $x^2 + 5x - 6 = ?$

   A. $x^2(5+6)$

   B. $x(x+5-6)$

   C. $(x+6)(x-1)$

   D. $(x+6)(x-6)$

17) Which of the following equations has a graph that is a straight line?

   A. $y = 3x^2 + 9$

   B. $x^2 + y^2 = 1$

   C. $4x - 2y = 2x$

   D. $7x + 2xy = 6$

18) What is the distance between the points (1, 3) and (−2, 7)?

   A. 3

   B. 4

   C. 5

   D. 6

19) Write the $\frac{4}{140}$ as a decimal.

A. 0.286

B. 286.00

C. 2.8600

D. 0.0286

20) Which of the following is one solution of this equation?

$x^2 + 2x - 5 = 0$

A. $\sqrt{6} - 1$

B. $\sqrt{2} + 1$

C. $\sqrt{6} + 1$

D. $\sqrt{2} - 1$

College–Level Mathematics

1) Solve the equation: $\log_4(x+2) - \log_4(x-2) = 1$

   A. 10

   B. $\dfrac{3}{10}$

   C. $\dfrac{10}{3}$

   D. 3

2) Solve $e^{5x+1} = 10$

   A. $\dfrac{\ln(10)+1}{5}$

   B. $\dfrac{\ln(10)-1}{5}$

   C. $5\ln(10) + 2$

   D. $5\ln(10) - 2$

3) If $f(x) = x - \dfrac{5}{3}$ and f^{-1} is the inverse of $f(x)$, what is the value of $f^{-1}(5)$?

   A. $\dfrac{10}{3}$

   B. $\dfrac{3}{20}$

   C. $\dfrac{20}{3}$

   D. $\dfrac{3}{10}$

4) What is cos 30°?

   A. $\frac{1}{2}$

   B. $\frac{\sqrt{2}}{2}$

   C. $\frac{\sqrt{3}}{2}$

   D. $\sqrt{3}$

5) If θ is an acute angle and sin θ = $\frac{3}{5}$, then cos θ = ?

   A. −1

   B. 0

   C. $\frac{4}{5}$

   D. $\frac{5}{4}$

6) What is the solution of the following system of equations?

$$\begin{cases} -2x - y = -9 \\ 5x - 2y = 18 \end{cases}$$

   A. (−1, 2)

   B. (4, 1)

   C. (1, 4)

   D. (4, −2)

7) Solve.

   |9 − (12 ÷ | 2 − 5 |)| = ?

   A. 9
   B. −6
   C. 5
   D. −5

8) If $\log_2 x$ = 5, then x = ?

   A. 2^{10}
   B. $\frac{5}{2}$
   C. 2^6
   D. 32

9) What's the reciprocal of $\frac{x^3}{16}$?

   A. $\frac{16}{x^3} - 1$
   B. $\frac{48}{x^3}$
   C. $\frac{16}{x^3} + 1$
   D. $\frac{16}{x^3}$

10) Find the inverse function for ln $(2x + 1)$

A. $\frac{1}{2}(e^x - 1)$

B. $(e^x + 1)$

C. $\frac{1}{2}(e^x + 1)$

D. $(e^x - 1)$

11) Simplify $(-5 + 9i)(3 + 5i)$.

A. $6 - 2i$

B. $60 - 2i$

C. $6 + 2i$

D. $-60 + 2i$

12) Find $\tan \frac{2\pi}{3}$

A. $-\sqrt{3}$

B. $\frac{\sqrt{3}}{2}$

C. $\sqrt{3}$

D. $\frac{1}{2}$

13) If f(x) = 3x − 1 and g(x) = x^2 − x, then find $(\frac{f}{g})(x)$.

A. $\frac{3x-1}{x^2-x}$

B. $\frac{x-1}{x^2-x}$

C. $\frac{x-1}{x^2-1}$

D. $\frac{3x+1}{x^2+x}$

14) What is the center and radius of a circle with the following equation?

$(x-5)^2 + (y+9)^2 = 3$

A. (5, 3), $\sqrt{3}$

B. (−9, 5), $2\sqrt{3}$

C. (5, −9), $\sqrt{3}$

D. (5, 9), $\sqrt{3}$

15) The slop of a line with the equation y = 8x + 10 is …

A. 10

B. 8

C. $\frac{8}{10}$

D. $\frac{10}{8}$

16) sin 2θ = ?

   A. 2 sin θ cos θ

   B. 2 sin θ

   C. 2 cos θ

   D. sin θ

17) If the center of a circle is at the point (−3, 2) and its circumference equals to 2π, what is the standard form equation of the circle?

   A. $(x - 3)^2 + (y + 2)^2 = 1$

   B. $(x + 3)^2 + (y - 2)^2 = 1$

   C. $(x + 6)^2 + (y - 6)^2 = 1$

   D. $(x - 3)^2 + (y - 2)^2 = 1$

18) If $sin\ A = \frac{1}{3}$ in a right triangle and the angle A is an acute angle, then what is $cos\ A$?

   A. $\frac{\sqrt{8}}{3}$

   B. $\frac{2}{3}$

   C. $\frac{\sqrt{3}}{8}$

   D. $\frac{\sqrt{8}}{9}$

19) Simplify $\dfrac{\sqrt{5}}{3\sqrt{20}}$

A. $\dfrac{\sqrt{5}}{6}$

B. $\dfrac{\sqrt{5}}{2}$

C. $\dfrac{1}{3}$

D. $\dfrac{1}{6}$

20) If $\log_{10} x = 2$, then $x = ?$

A. 2^{10}

B. 100

C. 20

D. $\dfrac{10}{2}$

ACCUPLACER Math Practice Test 1 Answer Key

❋ Now, it's time to review your results to see where you went wrong and what areas you need to improve!

Arithmetic and Elementary Algebra

1.	D	2.	A
3.	B	4.	C
5.	A	6.	A
7.	B	8.	A
9.	B	10.	C
11.	A	12.	B
13.	C	14.	C
15.	A	16.	C
17.	C	18.	B
19.	B	20.	A

College–Level Mathematics Test

1.	D	2.	B
3.	D	4.	A
5.	D	6.	B
7.	C	8.	D
9.	C	10.	B
11.	A	12.	C
13.	C	14.	C
15.	A	16.	D
17.	B	18.	C
19.	A	20.	C

www.EffortlessMath.com

ACCUPLACER Math Practice Test 2 Answer Key

Arithmetic and Elementary Algebra

1.	C	2.	A
3.	B	4.	D
5.	C	6.	B
7.	B	8.	B
9.	D	10.	D
11.	D	12.	B
13.	C	14.	A
15.	C	16.	C
17.	C	18.	C
19.	D	20.	A

College–Level Mathematics Test

1.	C	2.	B
3.	C	4.	C
5.	C	6.	B
7.	C	8.	D
9.	D	10.	A
11.	D	12.	A
13.	A	14.	C
15.	B	16.	A
17.	B	18.	A
19.	D	20.	B

ACCUPLACER Mathematics Practice Test 1 Answers and Explanations

Arithmetic and Elementary Algebra

1) **Choice D is correct**

Use FOIL (First, Out, In, Last)

$(x + 7)(x + 5) = x^2 + 5x + 7x + 35 = x^2 + 12x + 35$

2) **Choice A is correct**

$\frac{54}{6} = \frac{27}{3} = 9$, $\frac{48}{6} = \frac{24}{3} = 8$, $\frac{36}{6} = \frac{18}{3} = 6$, $\frac{59}{6} = \frac{59}{6}$ 59 is prime number

3) **Choice B is correct**

$x^2 - 81 = 0 \Rightarrow x^2 = 81 \Rightarrow x = 9$

4) **Choice C is correct**

If $a = 8$ then $b = \frac{8^2}{4} + 4 \Rightarrow b = \frac{64}{4} + 4 \Rightarrow b = 16 + 4 = 20$

5) **Choice A is correct**

If $6.5 < x \leq 9.0$, then x cannot be equal to 6.5

6) **Choice A is correct**

$a = 6 \Rightarrow$ area of triangle is $= \frac{1}{2}(6 \times 6) = \frac{36}{2} = 18$ cm

7) Choice B is correct

Simplify:

$10 - \frac{2}{3}x \geq 12 \Rightarrow -\frac{2}{3}x \geq 2 \Rightarrow -x \geq 3 \Rightarrow x \leq -3$

8) Choice A is correct

Factor each trinomial $x^2 - 2x - 8$ and $x^2 - 6x + 8$

$x^2 - 2x - 8 \Rightarrow (x - 4)(x + 2)$

$x^2 - 6x + 8 \Rightarrow (x - 2)(x - 4)$

9) Choice B is correct

$\frac{1+b}{6b^2} = \frac{1}{b^2} \Rightarrow (b \neq 0) \; b^2 + b^3 = 6b^2 \Rightarrow b^3 - 5b^2 = 0 \Rightarrow b^2(b - 5) = 0 \Rightarrow b - 5 = 0 \Rightarrow b = 5$

10) Choice C is correct

53° + 45° = 98°

180° − 98° = 82°

The value of the third angle is 82°.

11) Choice A is correct

$120 \times \frac{70}{100} = 84$

12) Choice B is correct

Solve for each equation:

(−1, 2)

$y = 1 - x \Rightarrow 2 = 1 - (-1) \Rightarrow 2 = 2$

$y = x + 1 \Rightarrow 2 = -1 + 1 \Rightarrow 2 \neq 0$

$x = -1 \Rightarrow -1 = -1$

$y = x + 3 \Rightarrow 2 = -1 + 3 \Rightarrow 2 = 2$

13) Choice C is correct

$(p^4) \cdot (p^5) = p^{4+5} = p^9$

14) Choice C is correct

If a = 8, then:

$4a^2 + 3a + 10 \Rightarrow 4(8)^2 + 3(8) + 10 \Rightarrow 4(64) + 24 + 10 = 290$

15) Choice A is correct

If $a^5 + b^5 = a^5 + c^5$

then:

$b^5 = c^5 \Rightarrow b = c$

16) Choice C is correct

$y = 5x - 3$

(1, 2) $\Rightarrow 2 = 5 - 3$ $\Rightarrow 2 = 2$

(−2, −13) $\Rightarrow -13 = -10 - 3$ $\Rightarrow -13 = -13$

(3, 18) $\Rightarrow 18 = 15 - 3$ $\Rightarrow 18 \neq 12$

(2, 7) $\Rightarrow 7 = 10 - 3$ $\Rightarrow 7 = 7$

17) Choice C is correct

$5^{\frac{7}{3}} \times 5^{\frac{2}{3}} = 5^{\frac{7}{3}+\frac{2}{3}} = 5^{\frac{9}{3}} = 5^3$

18) Choice B is correct

Underline the hundredths place:

152.6588

Look to the right if it is 5 or above, give it a shove.

Then, round up to 152.66

19) Choice B is correct

$a + b + c = 45$

$\frac{a+b+c+d}{4} = 20 \Rightarrow a + b + c + d = 80 \Rightarrow 45 + d = 80$

$d = 80 - 45 = 35$

20) Choice A is correct

$45 \times \$124 = \$5580$ Payable amount is: $\$8240 - \$5580 = \$2660$

College–Level Mathematics

1) **Choice D is correct**

$(g - f)(x) = g(x) - f(x) = (-x^2 - 1 - 2x) - (5 + x)$

$-x^2 - 1 - 2x - 5 - x = -x^2 - 3x - 6$

2) **Choice B is correct**

$\frac{|3 + x|}{7} \leq 5 \Rightarrow |3 + x| \leq 35 \Rightarrow -35 \leq 3 + x \leq 35 \Rightarrow -35 - 3 \leq x \leq 35 - 3 \Rightarrow$

$-38 \leq x \leq 32$

3) **Choice D is correct**

$$\tan\left(-\frac{\pi}{6}\right) = -\frac{\sqrt{3}}{3}$$

4) **Choice A is correct**

$$\frac{\sqrt{32a^5b^3}}{\sqrt{2ab^2}} = \frac{4a^2b\sqrt{2ab}}{b\sqrt{2a}} = 4a^2\sqrt{b}$$

5) **Choice D is correct**

$c(3) = (3)^2 + 10(3) + 30 = 9 + 30 + 30 = 69$

$4 \times 3 = 12 \Rightarrow 12 - 69 = -57 \Rightarrow 57{,}000$ loss

6) **Choice B is correct**

$$\sin B = \frac{\text{the length of the side that is opposite that angle}}{\text{the length of the longest side of the triangle}} = \frac{4}{5}$$

7) **Choice C is correct**

$$-7y = -6x - 12 \Rightarrow y = \frac{-6}{-7}x - \frac{12}{-7} \Rightarrow y = \frac{6}{7}x + \frac{12}{7}$$

8) **Choice D is correct**

E = 4 + A

A = S − 3

9) **Choice C is correct**

$\begin{cases} 5x + y = 9 \\ 10x - 7y = -18 \end{cases} \Rightarrow$ Multiplication (−2) in first equation $\Rightarrow \begin{cases} -10x - 2y = -18 \\ 10x - 7y = -18 \end{cases}$

Add two equations together $\Rightarrow -9y = -36 \Rightarrow y = 4$ then: $x = 1$

10) Choice B is correct

$(x - h)^2 + (y - k)^2 = r^2 \Rightarrow$ center: (h, k) and radius: r

$(x - 3)^2 + (y + 6)^2 = 12 \Rightarrow$ center: $(3, -6)$ and radius: $2\sqrt{3}$

11) Choice A is correct

If $z_1 = x_1 + iy_1$ and $z_2 = x_2 + iy_2 \Rightarrow \frac{z_1}{z_2} = \frac{x_1 x_2 + y_1 y_2}{x_2^2 + y_2^2} + i\frac{x_2 y_1 - x_1 y_2}{x_2^2 + y_2^2}$

In this problem: $x_1 = 4, x_2 = -3, y_1 = 0, y_2 = -4$

$\frac{4 - 3i}{-4i} = \frac{12}{16} + i\frac{16}{16} = \frac{3}{4} + i$

12) Choice C is correct

The number under the square root symbol must be zero or greater than zero therefore:

$x - 2 \geq 0 \Rightarrow x \geq 2$ domain of function $= [2, +\infty)$

13) Choice C is correct

$f(x) = \frac{x-2}{6} \Rightarrow y = \frac{x-2}{6} \Rightarrow 6y = x - 2 \Rightarrow 6y + 2 = x$

$f^{-1} = 6x + 2 = 2(3x+1)$

14) Choice C is correct

Set of number that are not composite between 1 and 25: A= {1, 2, 5, 7, 11, 13, 17, 19, 23}

$n(A) = 10 \Rightarrow p = \frac{10}{25} = \frac{2}{5}$

15) Choice A is correct

$e^{x-2} = 20 \Rightarrow \ln(e^{x-2}) = \ln(20)$

$(x - 2) \ln(e) = \ln(20)$

$x - 2 = \ln(20) \Rightarrow x = \ln(20) + 2$

16) Choice D is correct

METHOD ONE:

$\log_2(x+3) - \log_2(x-1) = 1$

Add $\log_2(x-1)$ to both sides: $\log_2(x+3) - \log_2(x-1) + \log_2(x-1) = 1 + \log_2(x-1)$

And simplify:

$\log_2(x+3) = 1 + \log_2(x-1)$

Logarithm rule: $a = \log_b(b^a) \Rightarrow 1 = \log_2(2^1) = \log_2(2)$

then: $\log_2(x+3) = \log_2(2) + \log_2(x-1)$

Logarithm rule: $\log_c(a) + \log_c(b) = \log_c(ab)$

then: $\log_2(2) + \log_2(x-1) = \log_2(2(x-1))$

$\qquad \log_2(x+3) = \log_2(2(x-1))$

When the logs have the same base: $\log_b(f(x)) = \log_b(g(x)) \Rightarrow f(x) = g(x)$

$x + 3 = 2(x-1) \quad \Rightarrow \quad x + 3 = 2x - 2 \quad \Rightarrow -x = -5 \Rightarrow x = 5$

METHOD TWO

We know that: $\qquad \log_a b - \log_a c = \log_a \frac{b}{c} \qquad$ and $\qquad \log_a b = c \Rightarrow b = a^c$

Then: $\log_2(x+3) - \log_2(x-1) = \log_2 \frac{x+3}{x-1} = 1 \Rightarrow \frac{x+3}{x-1} = 2^1 = 2 \Rightarrow x + 3 = 2(x-1)$

$\qquad \Rightarrow x + 3 = 2x - 2 \Rightarrow 2x - x = 3 + 2 \Rightarrow x = 5$

17) Choice B is correct

$\tan\theta = \frac{5}{12} \Rightarrow$ we have following triangle, then
$c = \sqrt{5^2 + 12^2} = \sqrt{25 + 144} = \sqrt{169} = 13$
$\cos\theta = \frac{12}{13}$

18) Choice C is correct

$C_3^8 = \frac{8!}{3!(8-3)!} = \frac{8!}{3!\,5!} = \frac{8 \times 7 \times 6 \times 5!}{3! \times 5!} = \frac{8 \times 7 \times 6}{3 \times 2 \times 1} = 56$

19) Choice is A correct

$$f(x) = \frac{6x-2}{3} \Rightarrow y = \frac{6x-2}{3} \Rightarrow 3y = 6x - 2 \Rightarrow 3y + 2 = 6x \Rightarrow \frac{3y+2}{6} = x$$

$$f^{-1} = \frac{3x+2}{6} \Rightarrow f^{-1}(2) = \frac{8}{6} = \frac{4}{3}$$

20) Choice C is correct

If two lines are parallel with each other, then the slope of the two lines is the same.
Then in line $y = 2x$, the slope is equal to 2
And in the line $2x - y = 4 \Rightarrow y = 2x - 4$, the slope equal to 2

ACCUPLACER Mathematics Practice Test 2 Answers and Explanations

Arithmetic and Elementary Algebra

1) **Choice C is correct**

Use FOIL (First, Out, In, Last)

$(x - 4)(x^2 + 5x + 4) = x^3 + 5x^2 + 4x - 4x^2 - 20x - 16$

$= x^3 + x^2 - 16x - 16$

2) **Choice A is correct**

Number of squares equal to: $\frac{54 \times 12}{3 \times 3} = 18 \times 4 = 72$

3) **Choice B is correct**

Simplify:

$7 + 2x \leq 15 \Rightarrow 2x \leq 15 - 7 \Rightarrow 2x \leq 8 \Rightarrow x \leq 4$

4) **Choice D is correct**

$\frac{a+b}{2} = 8 \quad \Rightarrow \quad a + b = 16$

$\frac{a+b+c}{3} = 9 \quad \Rightarrow \quad a + b + c = 27$

$16 + c = 27 \quad \Rightarrow \quad c = 27 - 16 = 11$

5) **Choice C is correct**

$7^7 \times 7^8 = 7^{7+8} = 7^{15}$

202

6) Choice B is correct

Underline the tenth place:

5231.48245

Look to the right if it is 5 or above, give it a shove.

Then, round up to 5231.5

7) Choice B is correct

$75 \times \dfrac{x}{100} = 15 \quad \Rightarrow \quad 75 \times x = 1500 \quad \Rightarrow \quad x = \dfrac{1500}{75} = 20$

8) Choice B is correct

$44 - $32.52 = $11.48

9) Choice D is correct

Simplify:

$$\dfrac{\dfrac{1}{2} - \dfrac{x+5}{4}}{\dfrac{x^2}{2} - \dfrac{5}{2}} = \dfrac{\dfrac{1}{2} - \dfrac{x+5}{4}}{\dfrac{x^2 - 5}{2}} = \dfrac{2(\dfrac{1}{2} - \dfrac{x+5}{4})}{x^2 - 5}$$

⇒ Simplify: $\dfrac{1}{2} - \dfrac{x+5}{4} = \dfrac{-x-3}{4}$

then: $\dfrac{2(\dfrac{-x-3}{4})}{x^2 - 5} = \dfrac{\dfrac{-x-3}{2}}{x^2 - 5} = \dfrac{-x-3}{2(x^2 - 5)} = \dfrac{-x-3}{2x^2 - 10}$

10) Choice D is correct

$\sqrt{47} = 6.85565...$

then: $\sqrt{47}$ is between 6 and 7

11) Choice D is correct

$55 \times \$77 = \$4235$ Payable amount is: $\$4265 - \$4235 = \$30$

12) Choice B is correct

$x_{1,2} = \dfrac{-b \pm \sqrt{b^2 - 4ac}}{2a}$

$ax^2 + bx + c = 0$

$4x^2 + 14x + 6 = 0 \quad \Rightarrow \quad$ then: a = 4, b = 14 and c = 6

$x = \dfrac{-14 + \sqrt{14^2 - 4.4.6}}{2.4} = -\dfrac{1}{2}$

$x = \dfrac{-14 - \sqrt{14^2 - 4.4.6}}{2.4} = -3$

13) Choice C is correct

$(x^6)^{\frac{5}{8}} = x^{6 \times \frac{5}{8}} = x^{\frac{30}{8}} = x^{\frac{15}{4}}$

14) Choice A is correct

$32 + 35 + 29 = 96$

Average $= \dfrac{96}{3} = 32$

15) Choice C is correct

$90° + 45° = 135°$

$180° - 135° = 45°$

16) Choice C is correct

$x^2 + 5x - 6 = (x - 1)(x + 6)$

17) Choice C is correct

$4x - 2y = 2x$ has a graph that is a straight line

18) Choice C is correct

$C = \sqrt{(x_A - x_B)^2 + (y - y_B)^2}$

$C = \sqrt{(1 - (-2))^2 + (3 - 7)^2}$

$C = \sqrt{(3)^2 + (-4)^2}$

$C = \sqrt{9 + 16}$

$C = \sqrt{25} = 5$

19) Choice D is correct

$\frac{4}{140} = \frac{1}{35} = 0.02857143 \cong 0.0286$

20) Choice A is correct

$x_{1,2} = \frac{-b \pm \sqrt{b^2 - 4ac}}{2a}$

$ax^2 + bx + c = 0$

$x^2 + 2x - 5 = 0 \quad \Rightarrow \quad$ then: $a = 1$, $b = 2$ and $c = -5$

$X = \frac{-2 + \sqrt{2^2 - 4 \cdot 1 \cdot -5}}{2 \cdot 1} = \sqrt{6} - 1 \qquad X = \frac{-2 - \sqrt{2^2 - 4 \cdot 1 \cdot -5}}{2 \cdot 1} = -1 - \sqrt{6}$

College–Level Mathematics Test

1) Choice C is correct

METHOD ONE

$\log_4(x+2) - \log_4(x-2) = 1$

Add $\log_4(x-2)$ to both sides

$\log_4(x+2) - \log_4(x-2) + \log_4(x-2) = 1 + \log_4(x-2)$

$\log_4(x+2) = 1 + \log_4(x-2)$

Apply logarithm rule: $a = \log_b(b^a) \Rightarrow 1 = \log_4(4^1) = \log_4(4)$

then: $\log_4(x+2) = \log_4(4) + \log_4(x-2)$

Logarithm rule: $\log_c(a) + \log_c(b) = \log_c(ab)$

then: $\log_4(4) + \log_4(x-2) = \log_4(4(x-2))$

$\log_4(x+2) = \log_4(4(x-2))$

When the logs have the same base: $\log_b(f(x)) = \log_b(g(x)) \Rightarrow f(x) = g(x)$

$(x+2) = 4(x-2)$

$x = \dfrac{10}{3}$

METHOD TWO

We know that: $\log_a b - \log_a c = \log_a \dfrac{b}{c}$ and $\log_a b = c \Rightarrow b = a^c$

Then: $\log_4(x+2) - \log_4(x-2) = \log_4 \dfrac{x+2}{x-2} = 1 \Rightarrow \dfrac{x+2}{x-2} = 4^1 = 4 \Rightarrow x+2 = 4(x-2)$

$\Rightarrow x + 2 = 4x - 8 \Rightarrow 4x - x = 8 + 2 \rightarrow 3x = 10 \Rightarrow x = \dfrac{10}{3}$

2) **Choice B is correct**

$e^{5x+1} = 10$

If $f(x) = g(x)$, then $\ln(f(x)) = \ln(g(x))$

$\ln(e^{5x+1}) = \ln(10)$

Apply logarithm rule: $\log_a(x^b) = b \log_a(x)$

$\ln(e^{5x+1}) = (5x+1)\ln(e)$

$(5x+1)\ln(e) = \ln(10)$

$(5x+1)\ln(e) = (5x+1)$

$(5x+1) = \ln(10) \quad\Rightarrow\quad x = \dfrac{\ln(10)-1}{5}$

3) **Choice C is correct**

$f(x) = x - \dfrac{5}{3} \quad\Rightarrow\quad y = x - \dfrac{5}{3} \Rightarrow y + \dfrac{5}{3} = x$

$f^{-1} = x + \dfrac{5}{3}$

$f^{-1}(5) = 5 + \dfrac{5}{3} = \dfrac{20}{3}$

4) **Choice C is correct**

$\cos 30° = \dfrac{\sqrt{3}}{2}$

5) **Choice C is correct**

$\sin\theta = \dfrac{3}{5} \Rightarrow$ we have following triangle, then

$c = \sqrt{5^2 - 3^2} = \sqrt{25-9} = \sqrt{16} = 4$

$\cos\theta = \dfrac{4}{5}$

6) Choice B is correct

$\begin{cases} -2x - y = -9 \\ 5x - 2y = 18 \end{cases} \Rightarrow$ Multiplication (–2) in first equation $\Rightarrow \begin{cases} 4x + 2y = 18 \\ 5x - 2y = 18 \end{cases}$

Add two equations together $\Rightarrow 9x = 36 \Rightarrow x = 4$ then: $y = 1$

7) Choice C is correct

$|9 - (12 \div |2 - 5|)| = |9 - (12 \div |-3|)| = |9 - (12 \div 3)| = |9 - 4| = |5| = 5$

8) Choice D is correct

METHOD ONE

$\log_2 x = 5$

Apply logarithm rule: $a = \log_b(b^a)$

$5 = \log_2(2^5) = \log_2(32)$

$\log_2 x = \log_2(32)$

When the logs have the same base: $\log_b(f(x)) = \log_b(g(x)) \Rightarrow f(x) = g(x)$

then: $x = 32$

METHOD TWO

We know that: $\log_a b = c \Rightarrow b = a^c$ $\qquad \log_2 x = 5 \Rightarrow x = 2^5 = 32$

9) Choice D is correct

$\dfrac{x^3}{16} \Rightarrow$ reciprocal is: $\dfrac{16}{x^3}$

10) Choice A is correct

$f(x) = \ln(2x + 1)$

$y = \ln(2x + 1)$

Change variables x and y: $x = \ln(2y + 1)$

solve: $x = \ln(2y + 1)$

$y = \dfrac{e^x - 1}{2} = \dfrac{1}{2}(e^x - 1)$

11) Choice D is correct

We know that: $\quad i = \sqrt{-1} \Rightarrow i^2 = -1$

$(-5 + 9i)(3 + 5i) = -15 - 25i + 27i + 45i^2 = -15 + 2i - 45 = 2i - 60$

12) Choice A is correct

$\tan\dfrac{2\pi}{3} = \dfrac{\sin\frac{2\pi}{3}}{\cos\frac{2\pi}{3}} = \dfrac{\frac{\sqrt{3}}{2}}{-\frac{1}{2}} = -\sqrt{3}$

13) Choice A is correct

$\left(\dfrac{f}{g}\right)(x) = \dfrac{f(x)}{g(x)} = \dfrac{3x - 1}{x^2 - x}$

14) Choice C is correct

$(x - h)^2 + (y - k)^2 = r^2 \Rightarrow$ center: (h, k) and radius: r

$(x - 5)^2 + (y + 9)^2 = 3 \Rightarrow$ center: $(5, -9)$ and radius: $\sqrt{3}$

15) Choice B is correct

$y = mx + b$

$m = slop$

$y = 8x + 10$

$m = 8$

16) Choice A is correct

$\sin 2\theta = 2\sin\theta\cos\theta$

17) Choice B is correct

$(x - h)^2 + (y - k)^2 = r^2 \Rightarrow$ center: (h, k) and radius: r

center: $(-3, 2) \Rightarrow h = -3, k = 2$

circumference = $2\pi \Rightarrow$ circumference = $2\pi r = 2\pi \Rightarrow r = 1$

$(x + 3)^2 + (y - 2)^2 = 1$

18) Choice A is correct

$\sin A = \frac{1}{3} \Rightarrow$ we have following triangle, then

$c = \sqrt{3^2 - 1^2} = \sqrt{9 - 1} = \sqrt{8}$

$\cos a = \dfrac{adjacent}{hypotenuse} \rightarrow \cos A = \dfrac{\sqrt{8}}{3}$

19) Choice D is correct

$\dfrac{\sqrt{5}}{3\sqrt{20}}$

$\sqrt{20} = 2\sqrt{5}$

$\dfrac{\sqrt{5}}{3 \cdot 2\sqrt{5}} = \dfrac{1}{6}$

20) Choice B is correct

METHOD ONE

$\log_{10} x = 2$

Apply logarithm rule: $a = \log_b(b^a)$

$2 = \log_{10}(10^2) = \log_{10}(100)$

$\log_{10}(100) = \log_{10} x$

When the logs have the same base: $\log_b(f(x)) = \log_b(g(x)) \Rightarrow f(x) = g(x)$

then: $x = 100$

METHOD TWO

We know that: $\log_a b = c \Rightarrow b = a^c$ $\log_{10} x = 2 \Rightarrow x = 10^2 = 100$

"Effortless Math Education" Publications

Effortless Math authors' team strives to prepare and publish the best quality ACCUPLACER Mathematics learning resources to make learning Math easier for all. We hope that our publications help you learn Math in an effective way and prepare for the ACCUPLACER test.

We all in Effortless Math wish you good luck and successful studies!

Effortless Math Authors

Made in the USA
Coppell, TX
29 January 2020